读后续写的
理论与实践

黄文藻　著

郑州大学出版社

图书在版编目(CIP)数据

读后续写的理论与实践/黄文藻著. — 郑州:郑州大学出版社,2022.8(2024.6 重印)

ISBN 978-7-5645-8783-3

Ⅰ. ①读… Ⅱ. ①黄… Ⅲ. ①英语 – 写作 – 教学研究 – 高中 Ⅳ. ①G633.412

中国版本图书馆 CIP 数据核字(2022)第 099668 号

读后续写的理论与实践

DUHOU XUXIE DE LILUN YU SHIJIAN

策划编辑	刘金兰	封面设计	苏永生
责任编辑	秦熹微	版式设计	苏永生
责任校对	呼玲玲	责任监制	李瑞卿

出版发行	郑州大学出版社	地　　址	郑州市大学路 40 号(450052)
出版人	孙保营	网　　址	http://www.zzup.cn
经　　销	全国新华书店	发行电话	0371-66966070
印　　刷	廊坊市印艺阁数字科技有限公司		
开　　本	710 mm×1 010 mm　1 / 16		
印　　张	12	字　　数	225 千字
版　　次	2022 年 8 月第 1 版	印　　次	2024 年 6 月第 2 次印刷

书　　号	ISBN 978-7-5645-8783-3	定　　价	68.00 元

本书如有印装质量问题,请与本社联系调换。

前 言

《普通高中英语课程标准》对英语写作教学规定了具体目标,在写作教学中培养学生的学科核心素养成为英语教学十分重要的环节。英语学科要给予学生未来发展所需要的正确价值观、关键能力和必备知识,其实质是让学生顺利建立完成学习、理解、应用、实践和迁移创新的学科认识活动和问题解决活动所需的稳定的心理机制,即学生的学科能力。高中英语的读后续写就是基于学习、理解、应用迁移的学科能力。

一、研究背景

新一轮高考英语命题改革对高中英语写作教学提出了更高的要求,读后续写是新高考英语试题的重要组成部分。在实际教学中,读后续写是困扰英语写作教学的难题,既是学生学习的难点,也是教师教学的难点。基于这样的认识,我们开展了关于读后续写的理论研究和教学实践,我们相信,这项研究一定能推动英语写作教学的进一步改进。

二、研究目的

读后续写的研究目的就是基于核心素养,探讨读后续写的理论起源,发现读后续写的写作规律,总结读后续写的写作模式,从而更好地为写作教学服务。

笔者在读后续写的理论和实践方面做了有益探索。首先基于课程标准,笔者和参与读后续写研究的教师通过对高考试题样本解读,认真分析了读后续写高考命题方向和新高考的最新变化,总结了读后续写的典型特征,提出读后续写语言能力培养的目标和方向。在实际教学过程中,笔者在认真总结前人理论基础上,提出了自己的新观点,并把这种新观点应用到实际教学中来,从而形成了读后续写课堂教学新模式。

三、研究设计

笔者围绕读后续写的理论和实践进行了下面的研究:

1. 读后续写理论起源;

2. 读后续写与核心素养;

3. 读后续写与高考命题;

4. 读后续写的课堂设计。

笔者和参与读后续写研究的教师根据课堂教学的实际情况,设计了13种读后续写的课程情景,这基本概括了读后续写高考命题的范畴。写作过程中语言能力的培养离不开写作手法和写作技巧,因此读后续写六种写作手法的运用也是笔者和参与读后续写研究的教师关注的一个方面。

重要的是,读后续写的主题语境是按照《普通高中英语课程标准》的要求进行设计和规划的。学生对主题语境的学习和探究是学习语言的重要的内容,这些内容直接影响学生语篇理解的程度、思维发展水平和语言学习的成效。笔者通过科学设计,让学生在人与自我、人与社会和人与自然这三大主题语境中,特别是在学会生活与学习、做人与做事、社会服务与人际沟通、安全防护、环境保护、探索自然等方面发展自我,完善自我,发展了英语学科的核心素养。笔者和参与读后续写研究的教师充分研究高考命题和《普通高中英语课程标准》,总结关于主题语境的八个重要话题。这样的课程设计更科学、更有效,对学生的核心能力的培养更有针对性。

在读后续写的实践过程中,笔者围绕提高语言能力方面也做了有益的探索。首先根据教学实际,笔者提出构建语料库,也就是建立本语境下的词汇短语、情景句式和语段,从微入手,循序渐进,帮助学生解决语言输入的根本问题,为下一步篇章写作做准备。其次,精心挑选话题句子,学生品味欣赏优秀句式奥妙的同时,也学会了使用优秀句式表达,提高了句子层次,写出了表达地道的好句式。

对于语篇的情节的设计,笔者首先以高考真题或各个省市的典型的模考试题为蓝本,从解读文本故事开始,分析三条线——时空线、情节线、情感发展线,这些是为故事情节的融洽做铺垫;再根据文本,分析关键人物以及性格,为续写故事做准备;最后多角度解读提示句,拓宽写作思路,尽可能使续写符合文本特点。

本研究对象是高中一年级到高中三年级的一个教学班的46名学生。选取这些学生的主要目的是分析实施读后续写课堂设计后对学生写作能力的影响,以及这些研究对象的读后续写的成绩对本研究的支撑因素的变量,以期望本研究对实际教学产生正相关。

本研究采用的方法是文献研究法。通过日常课堂教学,进一步探究读后续写的最佳课堂设计,持续改进教学方法,并与非研究班的情况对比,探索出行之有效的方法,得出科学结论。

四、研究价值

笔者对读后续写理论的研究达到了两方面的目的:一是丰富了读后续写理论的理论内涵;二是推动了读后续写的课堂教学。笔者希望这一研究成果能够激发更多的一线教师加入对读后续写的研究中来,共同完善学生英语学科能力的理论架构和实现途径;也希望这一成果可以帮助老师提高课堂的效率,经过更广泛和深入的实践,提升自身的专业素养。

在附录中,选取了部分参与研究的教师的读后续写的教案和课堂设计,选编的目的主要是抛砖引玉,给读者一点启发,相信广大教师设计出更有创意的读后续写的教案和课堂设计。笔者认为,在深入了解读后续写理论和课堂设计基本思路的基础上,充分发挥自己的创造性,便可逐步形成自己的课堂教学模式。

由于个人水平有限,也因为研究的时间短,可能出现一些错误,希望大家批评指正。

黄文藻

2022 年 1 月

目录

导　论　读后续写的理论基础

在研究人类交流交际的过程中,语言学研究人员 Atkinson,Pickering 和 Garrod 提出了互动协同模式(interactive alignment model)。根据这一理论,人们在交际过程中相互配合,相互适应,不断调整,双方大脑表征出现趋同或协同。这样的协同既发生在语言层面(语音、词汇、句法等),也体现在情境模式(situation model)层面。交际双方在互动中,相互协调情境模式,引发语言层面的协同,交流信息逐步理解。情境模式和语言表征的互动协同,使交际中的语言理解和语言产出紧密结合起来,信息顺畅交流。广东外语外贸大学外国语言学及应用语言学研究中心教授王初明最早提出了语言交流的互动协同理论,研究人员王敏认为协同实质是一种学习效应。

近几年来,语言学互动协同理论的研究在国内发展得很快,不少学者和研究人员提出了很有价值的观点。以互动协同模式为基础,王初明提出的外语学习的有效路径"互动—理解—协同—产出—习得"的观点在全国影响最大。王初明教授认为,理解与输出之间互动而催生协同效应,较弱的输出能力在与理解能力的协同中不断得到提高。因此,有效的语言习得植根于互动,经过输入、理解、协同、输出等环节而产生的协同效应。这就是英语教学中读后续写的理论基础。

姜琳、陈锦老师研究了读后续写对学习者语言准确性、复杂性和流利性发展的影响。他们认为,读后续写能够有效提升学习者语言产出的质量,特别是提高了语言准确性和复杂性。王初明教授提出读后续写任务可以提供连贯衔接的模式。续写能够促进文章内容,结构,语言和语篇连贯的完善。

传统的英语教学中,教师往往注重英语的知识点和语法,忽视英语本身的价值和意义。长期以来,英语写作教学没有将阅读与写作有机地结合起来,阅读与写作相脱节,影响了语言输入与输出的有效结合,从而影响了写作教学效果。王初明指出,外语学习效率的高低取决于语言理解和产出结合的紧密程度,两者结合产生协同效应;结合得越紧密,协同效应越强。协同是指所产出的语言与所理解的语言趋于一致。"读后续写"就是在这一理论背景下提出的,并为英语写作教学提供了新的思路和方法。

读后续写就是以协同效应作为理论基础的。这就表明,续写所用的语言和文本的语言在形式、风格、思想等方面应尽量保持一致。考生可以基于前文的阅读对自身运用的语言进行模仿,与前面的文本保持统一和一致,进而做到内容上的丰富和创新。

读后续写教学过程实际就是"语言输入—语言内化—语言输出"的过程。学习者阅读一篇没有结尾的文章,进行语言输入和语言内化,与故事情节和写作风格的一致性相衔接,最后补全文章的结尾完成语言输出。

读后续写为高中英语写作教学提供了新视野,以续促学可以加强阅读理解与写作产出的互动协同。在教学实践中,建立合理有效的阅读写作资源,教师有针对性地介入指导和动态评价方式会促进阅读和写作的效果,从而把学生的写作潜能挖掘出来,真正促进其英语写作水平的提高。

第一章 读后续写与《普通高中英语课程标准》

高中阶段是学生学习的重要阶段,也是学生核心素养发展的重要阶段。读后续写是培养学生阅读和写作能力的好方式,在英语学科中注重核心素养,可以有效促进学生的语言表达能力、学习能力、文化意识以及思维品质等各方面的全面提升。

第一节 读后续写与核心素养

高中英语学科核心素养主要包括语言能力、文化意识、思维品质和学习能力。读后续写能促进学生核心素养的发展。

一、语言能力

英语语言能力指在社会情境中,以听、说、读、看、写等方式理解和表达意义的能力,以及在学习和使用语言的过程中形成的语言意识和语感。英语语言能力构成英语学科核心素养的基础要素。实践表明,读后续写能促进读和写的能力,语言的流畅性、准确性和复杂性都有明显的提高。

二、文化意识

英语学习者的文化意识指对中外文化的理解和对优秀文化的认同,是学生在全球化背景下表现出的跨文化认知、态度和行为取向。文化意识体现英语学科核心素养的价值取向。学生在读后续写的过程中,培养了文化意识,增强了国家认同感和家国情怀,坚定了文化自信,逐步树立人类命运共同体意识,这为学生成长为有文明素养和社会责任感的人打下了基础,读后续写过程就是文化意识增强的过程。

三、思维品质

英语学习者的思维品质指思维在逻辑性、批判性、创新性等方面所表现出的能力和水平。思维品质体现英语学科核心素养的心智特征。学生在读后续写过程中,提升了分析和解决问题的能力,能够从跨文化视角观察和认识世界,对事物作出正确的价值判断。读后续写最大程度体现了逻辑性、批判性、创新性的思维品质。经过一定阶段的训练,学生在读后续写的过程中能自觉运用正确的价值观和思维品质。

四、学习能力

学习能力指学生积极运用和主动调适英语学习策略、拓宽英语学习渠道、努力提升英语学习效率的意识和能力。学习能力构成英语学科核心素养的发展条件。学生在读后续写过程中,培养了学习能力,养成了良好的学习习惯,能多渠道主动获取学习资源,并能自主、高效地开展学习。

第二节 读后续写课程内容设计

课程内容就是教材、学习活动和学习经验的集合。课程内容是根据课程标准设计,并按照一定的逻辑规律编排而成的知识体系,是师生在课堂上有效传递知识的重要途径。

英语课程内容是发展学生英语学科核心素养的基础,包含六个要素:主题语境、语篇类型、语言知识、文化知识、语言技能和学习策略。主题语境涵盖人与自我、人与社会和人与自然,涉及人文社会科学和自然科学领域等内容,为学科育人提供话题和语境。语篇类型为语言学习提供文体素材。语言知识涵盖语音知识、词汇知识、语法知识、语篇知识和语用知识,是构成语言能力的重要基础。文化知识是指中外优秀人文和科学知识,既包含物质文明知识,也包含精神文明知识,是学生形成跨文化意识、涵养人文和科学精神、坚定文化自信的知识源泉。学习策略包括元认知策略、认知策略、交际策略、情感策略等,有效选择和使用策略是帮助理解和表达、提高学习效率的手段,是学生形成自主学习和终身学习能力的必备条件。

课程内容的六个要素是一个相互关联的有机整体。所有的语言学习活动都应该在一定的主题语境下进行,即学生围绕某一具体的主题语境,基于不同类型的语篇,在解决问题的过程中,运用语言技能获取、梳理、整合语言知识和文化知识,深化对语言的理解,重视对语篇的赏析,比较和探究文化内涵,汲取文化精华;同时,尝试运用所学语言创造性地表达个人意图、观点和态度,并通过运用各种学习策略,提高理解和表达的效果,由此构成六要素整合、指向学科核心素养发展的英语学习活动观。

按照普通高中英语课程的内容要求和以上六大要素,读后续写的课程内容也必然体现主题语境、语篇类型、语言知识、文化知识、语言技能和学习策略所规定的学习内容及要求。读后续写的语篇包含人与自我、人与社会和人与自然三大主题内容。

一、主题语境

主题为语言学习提供主题范围或主题语境。学生对主题意义的探究应是学生学习语言的最重要内容,直接影响学生语篇理解的程度、思维发展的水平和语言学习的成效。人与自我、人与社会和人与自然这三大主题语境包含了中外文化的范畴,读后续写的教学设计应遵照普通高中英语课程的三大主题语境描述内容要求。

主题语境不仅规约着语言知识和文化知识的学习范围,还为语言学习提供意义语境,并有机渗透情感、态度和价值观。教师要认识到,学生对主题语境和语篇理解的深度直接影响学生的思维发展水平和语言学习成效。读后续写的过程是对主题意义探究的过程,在这一过程中,学生语言能力、文化意识、思维品质和学习能力得以融合发展。

在以主题意义为引领的读后续写的课堂上,充分挖掘特定主题所承载的文化信息和发展学生思维品质是关键。以解决问题为目的,整合语言知识和语言技能的学习与发展,将特定主题与学生的生活建立密切关联,鼓励学生学习和运用语言,提高学生的鉴别和评判能力;同时,通过中外文化比较,培养学生的逻辑思维和批判性思维,引导学生建构多元文化视角,丰富人生阅历和思维方式,树立正确的世界观、人生观和价值观,实现知行合一。

二、语篇类型

读后续写的语篇类型是记叙文,记叙文是学生常见的语篇形式,这种语篇分记人和叙事两种模式,都以丰富曲折的故事情节贯穿其中。故事情节的发展多包含背景、经过和结局。把握记叙文语篇的特定结构、文体特征和表达方式,有助于学生加深对语篇意义的理解。

教师在进行读后续写教学时,要认真研读和分析语篇,在引导学生挖掘主题意义的活动中,整合语言知识学习、语言技能发展、文化意识形成和学习策略运用,落实培养和发展学生英语学科核心素养的目标。

三、语言知识

语言知识包括语音、词汇、语法、语篇和语用知识。学习语言知识的目的是发展语言运用能力,因此要特别关注语言知识的表意功能。读后续写的特点要求教学过程中要特别关注词汇、语法、语篇和语用知识。

(一)词汇知识

读后续写是学习词汇的有效途径。语言学家 D. Awlkins 曾说过:"没有词汇就不能表达任何东西!"词汇是一种语言中所有词和词组的总和。词汇中的任何词语都是通过一定的句法关系和语义关系与其他词语建立起一定联系的,并在语境中传递信息。读后续写过程中,学习词汇不只是记忆词的音、形、义,更重要的是在语篇中理解和表达与各种主题相关的信息或观点,在语境中培养学生的词块意识,构建不同词汇语义网,并通过广泛阅读,进一步扩大词汇量,提高运用词汇准确理解和确切表达意义的能力。这一过程中强化语感,迁移词语运用能力,最终做到词语内化。在具体教学中,教师要引导学生利用词语的结构和文本的语境理解词语的意思,借助词典等资源,学习词语的用法,并大胆使用新的词语表达自己的意思。在学生词汇学习的过程中,教师可以根据主题,引导学生使用思维导图梳理词汇,科学有规律地记忆和学习词汇。

(二)语法知识

英语语法知识包括词法知识和句法知识:词法关注词的形态变化,如名词的数、格,动词的时、态(体)等;句法关注句子结构,如句子的成分、语序、种类等。词法和句法之间的关系非常紧密。在语言使用中,语法知识是"形式—意义—使用"的统一体,与语音、词汇、语篇和语用知识紧密相连,直接影响语言理解和表达的准确性和得体性。

读后续写的课程能让学生在具体语境中恰当地运用所学语法知识。在读后续写过程中,词汇、语法、语篇和语用知识总是交织在一起,成为语篇意义建构的最重要的基础。语法参与传递语篇的基本意义,语法形式的选择取决于具体语境中所表达的语用意义。据此,语法知识的使用不仅需要做到准确和达意,还要做到得体,因为读后续写语篇中的人物的意图、情感态度及其对具体语境下参与角色和身份的理解,这些都离不开语用意识和相关的语用知识。因此,在读后续写教学中,教师应重视在语境中呈现新的语法知识,在语境中指导学生观察所学语法项目的使用场合、表达形式、基本意义和语用功能,引导学生不断加强准确、恰当、得体地使用语言形式的意识。

(三)语篇知识

语篇是表达意义的语言单位。在使用语言的过程中,语言使用者不仅需要运用词汇和语法知识,而且需要将语言组织为意义连贯的语篇。这就需要运用语篇知识。语篇知识就是关于语篇是如何构成、语篇是如何表达意义以及人们在交流过程中如何使用语篇的知识。

语篇中各要素之间存在复杂的关系,如句与句、段与段、标题与正文之间的关系。这些关系涉及语篇的微观和宏观组织结构。句子内部的语法结构、词语搭配、指代关系、句子的信息展开方式等,属于语篇的微观组织结构。语篇中段与段的关系以及语篇各部分与语篇主题之间的关系,则属于语篇的宏观组织结构。

语篇知识有助于语言使用者有效理解读到的语篇。读后续写多为记叙性语篇,语篇中的段落主题句、话语标记语是记叙文的特征,学生把握记叙文的特征就可以明确文章的脉络,从而提高阅读效果。读后续写过程中,语篇知识有助于语言使用者根据交流的需要选择恰当的语篇类型、设计合理的语篇结构、保持语篇的衔接性和连贯性。

教师应该有意识地渗透有关语篇的基本知识,帮助学生形成语篇意识,把握语篇的结构特征,从而提高理解语篇意义的能力。同时,教师要引导学生充分利用语篇知识有效地获取和传递信息,表达观点和态度,达到与他人沟通和交流的目的。

(四)语用知识

语用知识指在特定语境中准确理解他人和得体表达自己的知识。掌握一定的语用知识有助于学生根据交际目的、交际场合的正式程度、参与人的身份和角色,得体且恰当地与他人沟通和交流,达到交际的目的。

语言的得体使用必须考虑参与者所处的语境。读后续写过程中,语言形式和语体风格会因交际场合的正式程度、行事程序、交际参与人身份的不同而不同。具体而言,语境主要涉及交际的时间、地点、情境等环境因素,也涉及参与人的交际目的、交际身份、处境及心情等个体因素。因此,在读后续写教学中,教师要增强语用意识,在设计读后续写教学活动时,努力创设接近真实世界的交际语境,明确交际场合、参与人的身份及其之间的关系,帮助学生认识到语言形式的选择受到具体交际情境的影响。

四、文化知识

文化知识包含中外文化知识,是学生在语言学习活动中理解文化内涵,比较文化异同,汲取文化精华,坚定文化自信的基础。掌握充分的中外多元文化知识,认同优秀文化,有助于促进英语学科核心素养的形成和发展。读后续写的过程就是学习中外优秀文化的过程。这有助于学生在对不同文化的比较、鉴赏、批判和反思的过程中,拓宽国际视野,理解和包容不同文化,增强对中华优秀传统文化的认同。

五、语言技能

语言技能是语言运用能力的重要组成部分。语言技能包括听、说、读、写等方面的技能。读后续写过程中"读"是理解性技能,"写"是表达性技能。理解性技能和表达性技能在语言学习过程中相辅相成、相互促进。

读后续写过程就是发展学生英语语言技能的过程。学生先通过读的过程,理解语篇所传递的信息、观点、情感和态度等;再利用所学语言知识、文化知识等创造新的语篇,这就是语言的输出。这些活动是学生发展语言能力、培养思维品质和学习能力的重要途径。

读后续写过程中,各种语言技能往往不是单独进行的,理解性技能与表达性技能是同时使用的。教师既要关注学生的具体技能训练,更要关注技能的综合运用。教师在读后续写过程中要选择贴近学生生活经验的主题语篇,激发学生参与学习和体验语言的兴趣,提高分析问题和解决问题、批判与创新的能力。

六、学习策略

学习策略主要指学生为促进语言学习和语言运用而采取的各种行动和步骤。学习策略表现为学生在语言学习和运用的活动中,受问题意识的驱动而采取的调控和管理自己学习过程的学习行为。有效的学习策略有助于提高学生学习英语的效果和效率,有助于学生发展自主学习的习惯和能力。

读后续写过程中,教师应培养学生的学习策略,有意识地引导学生学习并尝试使用各种不同的学习策略,并逐步形成适合自己的方法;教师要注意指导学生调控自己的情感,利用多种资源开展学习活动;帮助学生在语言实践活动中通过有效运用各种学习策略,提高分析语言和文本结构的能力、理解与沟通的能力以及创建文本的能力。

第二章 读后续写与高考命题

自王初明教授首次提出读后续写的协同理论后,读后续写受到英语教学界的持续关注。近几年来,我国英语界关于读后续写的研究逐渐开展起来。特别是 2016 年 10 月,浙江省率先在高考英语试卷中采用读后续写题型,这大大激发了研究人员和一线教师对读后续写理论的研究热情。

读后续写题型能有效考查学生的阅读和写作水平,区分度较高,并且能产生积极的教学效应。读后续写有效地促进学生英语学科综合性能力的提升,有效地增加英语学习能力和学习水平,促进传统英语教学模式的转变。随着读后续写理论的意义被逐渐认识,这为学生英语学习注入了新的活力,也为高中英语教师的教学提供了新方向和新视角。

读后续写的主要依据是协同理论。读后续写要求考生语言能力与提供的文本的语言融洽度高,并注重内容构思和情节衔接的能力。同时,读后续写赋予考生很大的理解和想象空间,发展了学生的思维品质,有助于考生对语篇结构的整体理解和把握。

第一节　高考命题方向

一、高考命题考查的策略

读后续写试题提供一段 350 词左右的文本材料,要求考生依据该材料内容、所给段落提示句进行续写,将其发展成一篇 150 词左右的短文。续写的短文要求与给定材料逻辑衔接、情节连贯、结构完整以及语言有较高的融洽度。语篇类型以记叙文或者夹叙夹议类的文章为主,故事情节较为曲折,故事线索的逻辑性比较强。这需要学生在阅读前文的基础上进行合理的构思和想象,对故事的发展持续推进,写出一个合情合理的结局。根据拉波夫叙事分析模式,续文的写作要重点关注故事后续的进展、结局、回应这三个方面内容,可以适当穿插评议。本试题满分 25 分。自 2016 年以来全国部分省、市读后续写试题如表 2-1 所示。

表 2-1　全国部分省、市读后续写试题

部分省、市高考年份	主题语境	话题
2021.6 新高考	人与自我	母亲节给妈妈惊喜
2021.1 浙江	人与自我	万圣节雕刻南瓜
2020.7 浙江	人与自然	遭遇北极熊
2019.12 山东模考	人与自然	收留可爱狗狗
2020.7 新高考	人与社会	帮助困难家庭
2020.1 浙江	人与自然	抚平狗狗心伤
2018.6 浙江	人与自我	度假骑马迷路
2017.11 浙江	人与自我	健忘妈妈趣事
2017.6 浙江	人与自然	骑行中途遇狼
2016.10 浙江	人与自我	吵架出走迷路

二、高考英语作文分数评价标准

(一)评分原则

(1)本题总分为 25 分,按 5 个档次给分。

(2)评分时,先根据所续写短文的内容和语言初步确定其所属档次,然后以该档次的要求来衡量、确定或调整档次,最后给分。

(3)词数少于 130 的,从总分中减去 2 分。

(4)评分时,应主要从以下四个方面考虑:

　　①与所给短文及段落开头语的衔接程度;

　　②内容的丰富性;

　　③应用语法结构和词汇的丰富性和准确性;

　　④上下文的连贯性。

(5)拼写与标点符号是语言准确性的一个重要方面,评分时,应视其对交际的影响程度予以考虑。

(6)如书写较差以致影响交际,可将分数降低一个档次。

（二）各档次的评分要求

高考英语书面表达题的具体评分要求如表2-2所示。

表2-2　各档次给分范围和要求

档次	评分要求
第五档 （21—25）	— 与所给短文融洽度高，与所提供各段落开头语衔接合理。 — 内容丰富，信息充分，最大限度表达文本意图。 — 所使用语法结构和词汇丰富、准确，可能有些许错误，但完全不影响意义表达。 — 有效地使用了语句间的连接成分，使所续写短文结构紧凑。
第四档 （16—20）	— 与所给短文融洽度较高，与所提供各段落开头语衔接较为合理。 — 内容比较丰富，信息较充分。 — 所使用语法结构和词汇较为丰富、准确，可能有些许错误，但不影响意义表达。 — 比较有效地使用了语句间的连接成分，使所续写短文结构紧凑。
第三档 （11—15）	— 与所给短文关系较为密切，与所提供各段落开头语有一定程度的衔接。 — 写出了若干有关内容，提供零星信息不完整。 — 应用的语法结构和词汇能满足任务的要求，虽有一些错误，但不影响意义的表达。 — 应用简单的语句间的连接成分，使全文内容连贯。
第二档 （6—10）	— 与所给短文有一定的关系，与所提供各段落开头语有一定程度的衔接。 — 写出了一些有关内容，提供信息不完整。 — 语法结构单调，词汇项目有限，有些语法结构和词汇方面的错误，影响了意义的表达。 — 较少使用语句间的连接成分，全文内容缺少连贯性。
第一档 （1—5）	— 与所给短文和开头语的衔接较差。 — 产出内容太少，只提供零星信息。 — 语法结构单调，词汇项目很有限，有较多语法结构和词汇方面的错误，严重影响了意义的表达。 — 缺乏语句间的连接成分，全文内容不连贯。
0	白卷、内容太少无法判断或所写内容与所提供内容无关。

三、高考命题考查内容

读后续写是将阅读和写作紧密结合的综合语言能力测试试题。读是输入，写是输出。输入的过程既要提取有效的文本信息，又要获取已经提供的文本的语言运用特点和风格。输出的过程是创造的过程,是将有效的文本信息组合,并且做出合乎逻辑的推测,使用和原文文本相一致的语言组织思维模式。

读后续写是一种将阅读与写作紧密结合的考查形式,旨在考查学生的综合语言运用能力。与应用文不同,读后续写除了要求学生掌握丰富的词汇和句式外,还注重学生的内容构思和情节衔接的能力。主要聚焦在以下四个方面,如图 2-1 所示。

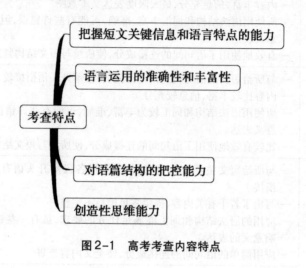

把握短文关键信息和语言特点的能力

语言运用的准确性和丰富性

考查特点

对语篇结构的把控能力

创造性思维能力

图 2-1　高考考查内容特点

四、高考命题方向

根据英语课程标准的要求,读后续写主要考查的主题语境如表 2-3 所示。

表 2-3　高考考查的主题语境

主题语境	主题群	重点考查的主题语境内容
人与自我	生活与学习,做人与做事	1. 个人、家庭、社区及学校生活 2. 健康的生活方式、积极的生活态度 3. 认识自我,丰富自我,完善自我 4. 优秀品行,正确的人生态度,公民义务与社会责任

续表2-3

主题语境	主题群	重点考查的主题语境内容
人与社会	社会服务与人际沟通	1. 良好的人际关系与社会交往 2. 公益事业与志愿服务 3. 跨文化沟通、包容与合作 4. 体育与健康、体育精神
人与自然	自然生态 环境保护 灾害防范	1. 自然环境、自然遗产保护 2. 人与环境、人与动植物 3. 自然灾害与防范,安全常识与自我保护

总体来看,读后续写主要考查学生在英语语言信息中发现问题、解决问题的能力,这是新课程标准核心素养的重要内容。

五、考生应对策略

1. 读懂原文是关键

由于选材多以记叙文、故事类文章或者夹叙夹议类的文章为主,考生首先要抓住记叙文的六要素(如图2-2所示),即(when、who、where、what、how、why)来提炼出文章的主旨。其次,弄清时空线、故事情节线和情感发展线。甄别利用文本中最有价值的信息。

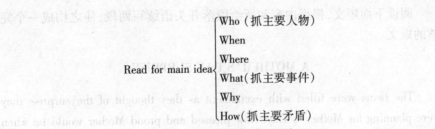

Read for main idea
Who(抓主要人物)
When
Where
What(抓主要事件)
Why
How(抓主要矛盾)

图2-2 英语记叙文的六要素

2. 理清文章脉络,构思故事情节

牢牢抓住故事发展的三条线:时空线、故事情节线和情感发展线。情节发展的依据是文本的信息和两个提示句。对于阅读段首提示句时,一定要针对提示句思考 why,what 和 how。只有这样做,才能理清命题者的意图是什么,也就能够理清故事的发展方向是什么,也只有这样才能确定合理的写作思路,创造出连贯合理的故事情节。

3. 根据构思情节，开始写作

①时态：以一般过去式为主。

②人称：看清是第一人称还是第二人称。

③语言：词汇的准确使用，句式结构的丰富多样，多描写，少平铺直叙。

④衔接：两段与前文的情节衔接，两个段落间的情节衔接，句与句之间的衔接。

特别注意：第一段的结尾一定要和第二段的提示句相衔接。

⑤连贯：在语言风格和故事的融洽度方面要与文本保持一致。

4. 定稿

写好初稿后，考生要结合文本中故事线索，仔细阅读自己续写的内容。既要确保不出现与原材料相矛盾的地方，又要做到内容上前后连贯，语句通顺。润色续写部分，使之过渡与衔接自然，尽量使用高级词汇，最好运用从句、独立主格结构、分词短语等高级句型。最后在誊写文字时，务必做到字迹工整和清晰。

第二节 高考试题样本分析

2021 新高考卷

阅读下面短文，根据内容和所给段落开头语续写两段，使之构成一个完整的短文。

A MOTHER'S DAY SURPRISE

The twins were filled with excitement as they thought of the surprise they were planning for Mother's Day. How pleased and proud Mother would be when they brought her breakfast in bed. They planned to make French toast and chicken porridge. They had watched their mother in the kitchen. There was nothing to it. Jenna and Jeff knew exactly what to do.

The big day came at last. The alarm rang at 6 a. m. The pair went down the stairs quietly to the kitchen. They decided to boil the porridge first. They put some rice into a pot of water and left it to boil while they made the French toast. Jeff broke two eggs into a plate and added in some milk. Jenna found the bread and put two slices into the egg mixture. Next, Jeff turned on the second stove burner to heat up the frying pan. Everything was going smoothly until Jeff started frying the bread. The pan was too hot and the bread turned black within seconds. Jenna threw the burnt piece into the sink and put in the other slice of bread. This time, she turned down the fire so it cooked nicely.

Then Jeff noticed steam shooting out of the pot and the lid starting to shake. The next minute, the porridge boiled over and put out the fire. Jenna panicked. Thankfully, Jeff stayed calm and turned off the gas quickly. But the store was a mess now. Jenna told Jeff to clean it up so they could continue to cook the rest of the porridge. But Jeff's hand touched the hot burner and he gave a cry of pain. Jenna made him put his hand in cold water. Then she caught the smell of burning. Oh dear! The piece of bread in the pan had turned black as well.

注意:

1. 续写词数应为 150 左右
2. 请按如下格式在答题卡的相应位置作答

As the twins looked around them in disappointment, their father appeared. The twins carried the breakfast upstairs and woke their mother up.

一、文本故事架构

本语篇属于"人与自我"——"生活与学习,做人与做事"主题语境下的"浓浓亲情 快乐家庭"话题。双胞胎 Jeff 和 Jenna 准备在母亲节为妈妈做法式吐司和鸡肉粥的早餐。故事体现了快乐家庭中的浓浓亲情。

（一）时空线

母亲节的早上,双胞胎在厨房为妈妈准备早餐。

（二）故事情节线

母亲节当天,双胞胎 Jeff 和 Jenna 给妈妈准备早餐,先煮粥,后把面包放进鸡蛋和牛奶的混合液中。由于火大,面包烤焦了。第二块面包将要烤成功之时,沸腾的粥把火熄灭了,厨房里一片狼藉,Jeff 的手也烫伤了,Jenna 帮他用冷水冲手的时候闻到了面包烧焦的味道。

（三）情感发展线

The twins were planning for Mother's Day surprise: prepared breakfast for mum. (confident)

↓

At 6 a. m,...the kitchen...Everything was going smoothly...(excited)

↓

Jeff started frying the bread…the bread turned black. (anxious)

↓

Jenna…cooked the other slice of bread…turned down the fire…(calm)

↓

Steam shooting out…the porridge boiled over and put out the fire. (panicked).

↓

Jeff turned off the gas quickly…the store was a mess…(calm)

↓

Jeff's hand touched the hot burner gave a cry of pain. (painful)

↓

Jenna put Jeff's hand in cold water…the noticed the piece turned black. (disappointed)

二、关键信息梳理

（一）人物

文本中的人物 4 个：Jeff、Jenna、father、mother。但最关键的人物应该是 twins：Jeff、Jenna。

文本中的关键词有：surprise, Mother's Day, the twins, excitement, make French toast and chicken porridge, a mess 等。这些词汇在续写故事情节的形成和发展过程中，起着非常重要的作用，抓住了这些关键词就抓住了续写的思路。

（二）提示句分析

根据第一段提示句"As the twins looked around them in disappointment, their father appeared"我们可以推断出，第一段主要写在紧急情况下，爸爸出现了如何帮助双胞胎完成为妈妈准备的早餐。

根据第二段提示句"The twins carried the breakfast upstairs and woke their mother up"我们可以推断出双胞胎端着早餐上楼，然后叫醒妈妈。主要写妈妈看到早餐后的反应和母子之间的互动。回应文本前文妈妈看到早餐"How pleased and proud Mother would be when they brought her breakfast in bed"的心情。

三、写作思路构建

双胞胎失望地看看四周，这时爸爸出现了。爸爸嘱咐他们不要慌张！然后帮 Jeff 和 Jenna 收拾残局并且教做早餐。在爸爸的指导下，孩子们成功了。爸爸高兴地为双胞胎竖起大拇指,然后跟开玩笑:做饭看来要多实践啊! 看到自己的成果,双胞胎也非常得意。

Jeff 和 Jenna 端着做好的早餐上了楼,叫醒了妈妈。妈妈看到孩子们做的早饭,先是困惑,后又惊讶,"你俩做的早饭?"Jeff 和 Jenna 得意地点点头并开心地笑了。爸爸在一旁也附和说 Jeff 和 Jenna 长大了! 妈妈非常高兴和自豪,这是妈妈过得最好的母亲节,高兴又充满了惊奇。

(一)习作欣赏

As the twins looked around them in disappointment, their father appeared. "Don't panic!" he handed each one a wet towel, helping them clean the mess quickly. After that, Jeff revealed their plan in a broken voice, his face flushing. However, Father laughed, "Sounds great! I can teach you to cook." At this, Jenna and Jeff almost jumped to their feet, joy in eyes. Under his careful guidance, it didn't take long before the French toast and chicken porridge were ready. Everything settled, Father left the kitchen, promising to keep their secret.

The twins carried the breakfast upstairs and woke their mother up. Meeting their smiling eyes, Mother felt confused until they presented the breakfast and said "Happy Mother's Day". Mother gave them a tight hug, "Unbelievable! You can cook! It's the biggest surprise I have received." Her face lit up with happiness. "They have known how to take care of others." Father said in response to her excitement, winking at Jenna and Jeff. They couldn't help giggling. It was a secret only shared between them.

(二)习作评价

"'Don't panic!' he handed each one a wet towel, helping them clean the mess quickly"这句话的语言和动作体现了爸爸在孩子们危急时刻的作用。而"Jeff revealed their plan in a broken voice, his face flushing"一句话,形象地刻画了双胞胎的窘况。接下来经过爸爸的指导早餐做成了。"'Unbelievable! You can cook! It's the biggest surprise I have received.' Her face lit up with happiness"这句话妈妈的惊喜之情溢于言表,突出了本文的主题。

第三节　语言能力培养

读后续写对语言能力的培养有很大作用。高考阅卷过程中,除故事情节和语篇结构外,阅卷人在评卷过程中最看重的是考生的语言表达能力。

实际上,写作中好的句子,总给阅卷老师眼前一亮的感觉,优秀地道的表达会增加写作的亮点,博得阅卷老师的青睐。怎样的语言才算好的表达?哪些表达会得到阅卷老师的青睐?

下面这些来自高考读后续写试题中摘录的考生写出的句子,是阅卷老师认可的优秀句式,这也是学生语言能力培养的方向。

一、使用形容词和形容词短语

在表达情感,描写心理活动时,形容词和形容词短语的使用,往往细致入微地刻画了人物形象,起着画龙点睛的作用。

①"Unbelievable! You can cook! It's the biggest surprise I have received."(2021 年全国新高考 I)

②Relieved yet exhausted, I climbed into the helicopter, hugging tightly with Elli. (2020 年 7 月浙江高考)

③Nose twitching with mouth wide open, he slammed on the broken fence madly with his powerful paws. (2020 年 7 月浙江高考)

④Amazed but cautious, Poppy stepped back a little. (2020 年 1 月浙江高考)

⑤We had no idea where we were and it got dark. Exhausted and hungry, I wondered if we could find our way back. (2018 年浙江高考范文)

⑥But no more helicopters came and it was getting dark again. Desperate and hopeless, Jane knelt down, tears streaming down her face. (2016 年浙江高考)

二、使用副词

在动作描写方面,或者表达情感等方面,副词的使用往往非常生动。

①Immediately, the house became the sea of happiness. (2020 年 1 月浙江高考)

②Naturally, he threw himself into his parents' arms and hugged them tightly. (2020 年 1 月浙江高考)

③The boy raised his head and surprisingly found the other beside a box watching him. (2020 年 1 月浙江高考)

④But no more helicopters came and it was getting dark again. Immediately, an absolute darkness ruled the forest. (2016 年浙江高考)

三、运用非谓语

非谓语动词是英语语言的重要语法现象,是句子的附属成分,是文意的有益补充。考生若能恰当使用,一定能凸显考生的语言运用能力。

①After that, Jeff revealed their plan in a broken voice, his face flushing. (2021 年全国新高考 I)

②Everything settled, Father left the kitchen, promising to keep their secret. (2021 年全国新高考 I)

③The angry bear rushed straight towards the leftovers of our dinner, leaving us precious time to escape the narrow camp. (2020 年 7 月浙江高考)

④Sunshine poured on the bear's fur, painting it with lovely golden colour. (2020 年 7 月浙江高考)

⑤Time went by swiftly, and the children laughed, carrying out their great "project". (2020 年山东高考)

⑥Carrying all the paper bags, he called out, "Popcorn! 50 cents for one extra-large pack!" (2020 年山东高考)

⑦Wrapped by their barking, the parents smiled in relief. (2020 年 1 月浙江高考)

⑧But no more helicopters came and it was getting dark again. Feeling disappointed, Jane had to stay alone for another night. (2016 年浙江高考)

四、运用 With 短语和 With 构成的独立主格结构

这种结构是英语中的最典型、最常用的结构,使用起来非常生动、形象和地道。

①At this, Jenna and Jeff almost jumped to their feet, joy in eyes. (2021 年全国新高考 I)

②With a loud bang, the beast fell down. (2020 年 7 月浙江高考)

③With the bear chasing behind, "Elli, come on," I yelled. (2020 年 7 月浙江高考)

④With a cracking noise, the bear rushed in, approaching us rapidly. (2020 年 7 月浙江高考)

⑤With little weapon to defend ourselves in this temporary camp, Eilli and I were nearly dead with fright. (2020 年 7 月浙江高考)

五、善于运用各种从句和关联词

从句和关联词的使用可以使文章逻辑紧密,上下文流畅,衔接自然。正确使用关联词会使语言的层次性更高。

①Under his careful guidance, it didn't take long before the French toast and chicken porridge were ready. (2021 年全国新高考 I)

②A chill spreading down my spine, what we could do was lying down and praying. (2020 年 7 月浙江高考)

③I was trapped to a narrow corner, where I could almost hear the gasps of the bear. (2020 年 7 月浙江高考)

④It was such a breathtaking experience, but as I developed the film later, it all just became worthwhile. (2020 年 7 月浙江高考)

⑤It turned out that their efforts not only helped a brother in need, but also gave themselves the sweet taste of helping others. (2020 年山东高考)

⑥She reached out her paw to investigate the puppy while the little creature shot its head out, exchanging cheerful greetings with her. (2020 年 1 月浙江高考)

六、运用介词以及介词的复合结构

写作中介词的合理使用,会使得语言更简洁,更生动。

①Father said in response to her excitement, winking at Jenna and Jeff. (2021 年全国新高考 I)

②We tried pepper spray again, but in vain. (2020 年 7 月浙江高考)

③Suddenly, a huge shadow pounced on us without mercy. (2020 年 7 月浙江高考)

④To our surprise, the bear rushed straight towards the leftovers of our dinner. (2020 年 7 月浙江高考)

⑤At the same time, John went to purchase some paper bags and arranged all the stuff in place. (2020 年山东高考)

⑥Within no time, Bernard sold out all popcorn and earned quite some money. (2020 年山东高考)

⑦On returning, he thanked the Meredith family with watery eyes. (2020 年山东高考)

七、多个动词连用

动词是英语的核心和灵魂,恰当、准确地使用动词以及动词的形式是考生语言运用能力的最重要的标志。

①We paced back, looked straight into his eyes and pretended not to be afraid.（2020 年 7 月浙江高考）

②We quickly packed our baggage, boarded the helicopter and finally breathed a sigh of relief.（2020 年 7 月浙江高考）

八、动作描写

通过使用恰当的副词、形容词以及从句来描写动作,这会使文章生动、形象、有立体感。

①However, a heavy growl quickly caught us up before we could secure a safe shelter.（2020 年 7 月浙江高考）

②With two bloodshot swollen eyes, he let out a deafening roar, charged at the fence and shoved the mesh with his full strength.（2020 年 7 月浙江高考）

③With cheerful barks, Poppy twisted her body dramatically, bouncing up to the height of the boy's knees, constantly licking his hand.（2020 年 1 浙江高考）

九、运用倒装句以及其他句型

倒装句或其他重要句式的使用会使得语言生动、地道。

①Strange it might seem, she suddenly turned around and ran away.（2020 年 1 月浙江高考）

②No sooner had he bent down to give Poppy a bear hug than happy kisses rained upon his face.（2020 年 1 月浙江高考）

③Had it not been for the staff's timely shot, we might not have survived under the bear's massive paws.（2020 年浙江高考）

④The manager explained that it was the climate change that forced polar bears into such hungry situation.（2020 年浙江高考）

⑤We have no alternative but to anxiously wait for the helicopter.（2020 年浙江高考）

十、恰当对话

直接引语的使用,给文章提供了画面感,立体感。

①"Don't panic!" Father comforted us.（2021 年全国新高考 I）

②She nodded with a smile and encouraged the children, "Let's get started!"（2020 年山东高考）

③"Let's see who gets there first!" Rachel shouted, as she pedaled fast and zoomed past Jenny. (2017 年浙江高考)

④"Hold on tight!" My father yelled. (2018 年浙江高考)

⑤The car abruptly stopped in front of him. "Get into the car." Paul shouted at Mac. (2017 年浙江高考)

十一、情绪渲染

情绪描写有助于增加文章的情感成分,表现人物的喜怒哀乐。

①They couldn't help giggling. It was a secret only shared between them. (2021 年全国新高考 I)

②The air was rich with happiness and kindness. (2020 年全国新高考)

③Meanwhile, a warm glow of satisfaction appeared on Poppy's face. (2020 年 1 月浙江高考试题)

④The moment she saw how she did for her Science test, tears started welling up in Tina's eyes and falling down her cheeks.

十二、运用比喻拟人等修辞手法

恰到好处地运用各种修辞手法,不仅可使语言更鲜活、具体、逼真,也能极大增强语言的艺术表现力和感染力。

①Gradually, Poppy calmed down and watched the little dog with tenderness, as if she were a dedicated mother. (2020 年 1 月浙江高考)

②He dashed into the house like an arrow and shouted in a cheerful voice: "Mom, Dad, Poppy!" (2020 年 1 月浙江高考)

③We drove through several states and saw lots of fanatic sights along the way. I looked out of the car window, winding rivers, lofty mountains, sunny beaches and deep valleys holding me entirely in their fascination. (2017 年 11 月浙江高考)

十三、巧妙设计问句

恰当使用问句,引起读者的强烈兴趣,增加文采。

①The next day we remembered the brand-new tent we had brought with us. Dad exchanged a glance with me. Why not camp to satisfy Mom? (2017 年浙江高考)

②Have you ever been on a self-driving trip? Let me tell you an exciting trip my family took this summer.

③Why does trouble always follow me around? Do I have a "kick me" sign on my back or something?

　　语言能力的培养不仅仅局限上述方面,实际教学中,还有很多优秀句式。在学习和使用语言的过程中形成的语言意识和语感也是非常重要的方面。英语语言能力构成了英语学科素养的基本要素,在读后续写的过程中,要善于把握语言能力的基本要素,全方位地培养学生的语言能力。

第三章 读后续写的情景设计

第一节 高兴兴奋

高兴、兴奋的心理特征是读后续写中常见的情景。这种心理活动常常和身体语言描写结合,如果再恰当地增加直接引语,就会生动形象地刻画出高兴、兴奋的画面。

一、构建语料库

(一)词汇短语

1.单词

amuse	v.给……提供娱乐/消遣;逗……乐	enjoy	v.喜爱;享受;欣赏
amused	adj.愉快的;开心的	joy	n.欢乐;高兴 乐趣
amusing	adj.逗乐的;有趣的	laugh	v.笑 n.笑;笑声
cheer	n.欢呼声 v.欢呼;(为……)喝彩;(使)振奋	merry	adj.愉快的;欢快的
cheerful	adj.兴高采烈的;高兴的	overjoyed	adj.极为高兴的;十分开心的
delight	n.快乐;高兴;乐事;v.使高兴;使欣喜	overcome	vt.战胜;使受不了;(感情等)压倒
emotion	n.感情;激情	pleasure	n.快乐;乐事;乐趣

2.词组

be full of emotion	充满激情
be enthusiastic about (doing) sth.	对(做)某事很有热情
be wild with joy	狂喜

be/feel in the mood for sth.	有做某事的心情
burst into laughter	放声大笑起来
cheer up	(使)振作起来;(使)高兴起来
for pleasure	作为消遣
in a good/bad mood	心情好/心情坏
in high / cheerful spirits	精神高涨的
jump for joy	高兴得跳起来
to one's joy/pleasure/enjoyment/satisfaction…	令人高兴的是
wear a shining smile	面带微笑
with satisfaction/surprise	满意地/惊讶地

(二)话题情景

①Father was wild with joy/delight. 父亲欣喜若狂。

②I was pleased beyond description. 我高兴得难以形容。

③She wore a shining smile on herface. 她脸上带着灿烂的笑容。

④Her smile lit up the whole room. 她的微笑点燃了整个房间。

⑤The smile on her face shone like a diamond.
她脸上的笑容像钻石一样闪闪发光。

⑥A smile of understanding flashed across his face.
他脸上闪过一抹理解的微笑。

⑦My face was shining with indescribably wild joy.
我的脸上闪着难以形容的狂喜。

⑧Her eyes shone/danced with pleasure.
她的眼睛高兴地闪闪发光/闪烁着。

⑨Unforgettable were her eyes that shone like diamonds and lips held in a
steady smile.
难忘的是她的眼睛,像钻石一样闪闪发光,嘴唇始终保持着微笑。

⑩Because of that smile,our hearts jump and dance for joy,sweet from the
heart filling the body.
因为那一笑,我们的心兴奋地怦怦直跳,从内心感到了甜蜜。

(三)情景语段

I was announced to be the winner. Trembling with enormous excitement, I
could scarcely believe it. Great applause wrapping me, a flood of pride weld up

inside. The moment the bell rang, I rushed out at the highest speed as I could. The road towards home had never seemed so long! By the time I entered my home, I threw myself into mom's arms and told her the good news. With eyes sparkling like diamonds, she kissed me on my forehead, showing her great encouragement.

二、语篇分析

阅读下面短文,根据内容和所给段落开头语续写两段,使之构成一个完整的短文。

After a very long wait, Mother and I was relieved to see our dog delivered 6 puppies! The sixth was the smallest and spotted black and white. I named her "Precious". I picked her up and laid her on top of the large pile of puppies, who were trying to nurse on the mother. Mother dog immediately pushed Precious away from rest of the group. She refused to recognize Precious as a member of her family.

"Something's wrong," said Mother.

I reached over and picked up Precious. My heart sank when I saw the little puppy had a harelip(兔唇) and could not close its little mouth. Precious would die because it could not suckle(吸吮).

I purchased a syringe (注射器) and fed Precious by hand. I did this every day and night, for more than ten days. The little puppy survived and learned to eat on her own as long as it was soft canned food.

Vacation was over and my new school life would begin. So I placed an ad for the puppies on the internet. Within several days, all had been picked up by their new families, except Precious. I decided to keep her and give her operation if my parents saved enough money.

That night at around seven-thirty, Mother and I were eating supper when we heard a knock on the front door. When I opened the door, there was a lady with her son standing behind. I explained to her there were no puppies left.

Just at that moment, Precious left in the bedroom began to bark.

"My puppy! My puppy!" yelled the little boy as he ran out from behind his mother.

I just about fell over when I saw that the small child also had a harelip.

The boy ran past me as fast as he could, down the hallway to where the puppy was still barking. Holding the puppy in his arms tightly, he looked up at his mother and said, "Look, mummy. They found homes for all the puppies except the pretty one, and he looks just like me!"

注意：

1. 续写词数应为 150 左右

2. 请按如下格式在答题卡的相应位置作答

> The boy bent there pressing Precious against his cheek.
>
> One year later, that boy with Precious came to me.

三、文本故事架构

本文属于"人与自然"——"人与动物"主题语境。家中初生的小狗宝贝有唇裂，狗狗妈妈抛弃了她，也没人愿意领养她。有位女士带着唇裂的男孩来领养了宝贝，并且认为是最漂亮的狗狗。文章体现了小男孩和作者热爱动物的情怀。考生在阅读这类文本时，应把握故事发展的三条线，即时空线、故事情节线和情感发展线。

（一）时空线

Mother dog refused to recognize the smallest Precious as a member of her family→My heart sank when I saw Precious had a harelip(兔唇)→I fed Precious by hand. I did this every day and night, for more than ten days→My new school life would begin so I placed an ad for the puppies on the internet→All had been picked up by their new families, except Precious→I decided to keep her→A lady with her son accepted her and her son thought she's the pretty one 等。

（二）故事情节线

家中的狗狗生了六只小狗，最后生的那只小狗狗，形体最小，我给她起名宝贝。但是她生来就是唇裂，狗妈妈也不把她看作家中的一员。宝贝不能自己吃奶，没人照料她不会活下来的。于是我买了注射器，每天亲自喂养她。开学了，我在互联网上发布领养狗狗的消息，但这只唇裂的小狗，没人愿意领养。晚上吃饭的时间，有位女士带着男孩要来领养狗狗，我正要说着狗狗全被认领了，这时无人愿意领养的宝贝开始叫起来，小男孩急忙跑过去抱住了她，并且说这只狗狗真像自己，是最漂亮的狗狗，于是领养了这只有唇裂的狗狗。

（三）情感发展线

狗妈妈生育 6 只小狗，最小的是 Precious(兴奋)→狗妈妈抛弃有唇裂的 Precious(心情沉重)→买工具人工喂养(爱护)→新学年开始，发互联网广告找领养(不忍心)→Precious 无人领养,自己养育并打算给她动手术(挚爱)→有唇裂的小男孩领养了 Precious(欣慰)。

四、关键信息梳理

(一)人物

语篇出现了 4 个人物。但关键的是唇裂的男孩、狗狗 Precious 和"我"。

文本中的关键词有:Precious,harelip,puppy,operation 和 the pretty one 等。这些词汇在续写故事情节的形成和发展过程中,起着非常重要的作用,抓住了这些关键词就抓住了续写的思路。

(二)提示句分析

第一段,小男孩蹲下身体,抱住狗狗,亲着自己的脸。这一段主要是描写小男孩对这只狗狗的依恋,他认为这只畸形的狗狗最漂亮,把他的心理活动描写出来,再写小男孩因为宝贝的陪伴,自己快乐生活。

第二段,一年之后,小男孩又带着狗狗来回访"我"。这一段主要是小男孩对"我"的感激和感恩,"我"也发现小男孩和狗狗的唇裂都做了手术,成为漂亮的一对宝贝。

五、写作思路构建

小男孩蹲下身体,抱住狗狗,狗狗热情地亲着他的脸。他低声地和狗狗交流着,不时用手抚摸着狗狗的毛发。孩子央求妈妈领养了宝贝。从此这一对快活地生活着,每天都一起散步生活。一年之后,小男孩又带着宝贝来回访我。我特别惊讶地发现小男孩和宝贝的唇裂不见了! 小男孩告诉我,妈妈攒够了足够多的钱,同时给他们做了手术。他们现在仍然是快乐的一对宝贝。小男孩特别感谢我让他拥有了宝贝,宝贝对小男孩来说是真正的"宝贝",让他度过了艰难的时光。

(一)习作欣赏

The boy bent there pressing the small puppy against his cheek. Seemingly understanding what was happening, "the pretty one" kissed the boy again and again. I even saw the bright smiles on his face. "They are the perfect pair!" I thought. Moved by the warm scene deeply, I decided to give the puppy for free when the mother inquired prices, through I was so devoted to my puppy! When they bid farewell with the dog to me, I hoped the pair could have a warm and happy life.

One year later, that boy with the dog came to me. Precious rushed to me the moment he saw me. Imagined how surprised I was to notice their harelip disappeared! After hearing their story, I understood he came to me specially to express his gratitude. "The pretty one" really gave him the happiness and lifted him up in the hard time. "We are in one!" The boy said, holding the puppy tightly. Any worries I'd had about the puppy's future were gone. The image of the little boy and his matching puppy stayed with me still.

（二）习作评价

续写部分用词较为地道，情节简洁紧凑，兴奋、高兴的情感表达更加生动，"They are the perfect pair!""We are in one!"等直接引语的使用，让兴奋之情溢于言表。

第二节　激动感动

激动、感动的心理特征是读后续写故事中常见的情景。这种心理活动常常和身体语言描写结合，如果再恰当地增加直接引语，就会生动形象地刻画出感动的画面。

一、构建语料积累

（一）词汇短语

1. 单词

affect	vt. 影响；感动	moved	adj. 感动
emotional	adj. 情绪（上）的；情感（上）的	touched	adj. 感动
excited	adj. 激动的	thrill	v. 使激动 n. 激动；引起激动的事物
inspire	v. 激发，鼓舞		

2. 词组

be excited with/over/about	为……而激动（兴奋）
be inspired by	受……的鼓舞
be moved to tears	感动流泪
heart melted	心被融化
hold back one's tears	控制住泪水

（二）情景句式

①Tears welled up in her eyes. 眼泪夺眶而出。

②A warm current rose in her heart. 一股暖流涌上心头。

③He was so thrilled that he could hardly speak. 他很激动，说不出话来。

④She could hardly contain her excitement. 她几乎掩饰不住自己的兴奋。

⑤Both Mark and I are feeling on the top of the world.
马克和我都觉得自己站在世界之巅。

⑥The children were filled with joy at the sight of the Christmas tree.
一看到圣诞树，孩子们就无比高兴。

⑦Hearing the news, he jumped up and down with excitement.
听到消息，他高兴地跳了起来。

⑧The players jumped for joy when he scored the winning goal.
当他赢得获胜一球的时候，队员们兴奋地跳了起来。

⑨A slow smile worked its way across his face and into his eyes.
浅浅的微笑爬上他的脸，融进他的眼睛中。

⑩As Susan bent her head, she heard the remark and she wiped away tears.
当 Susan 低下头时，她听到了这句话，擦去了眼泪。

（三）情景语段

When I arrived home, I found my mom preparing a grand dinner for my birthday party. A warm current welled up in my mind at the sight of all those delicate meals. I was not sure how much time she spent on the great party and her busy figure sent me completely in tears. "I love you, mom!" I threw myself into her arms and conveyed my thanks emotionally.

二、语篇分析

阅读下面短文，根据内容和所给段落开头语续写两段，使之构成一个完整的短文。

Love Will Melt Your Heart

The day before my daughter Noah's fourth birthday, something she said forecast a remarkable event. I had just picked her up from preschool when she cautioned me to mind the elderly person walking across the parking lot at a glacier' space. She went on to explain that she has a soft spot for mature folks: "I like old people the best because they walk slow like I do and they have soft skin like me. They all going to die soon, so I'm going to love them before they die."I was struck by her thoughtfulness and empathy.

The following day—her birthday—again on the way home from school, she asked if we could stop at the grocery store to buy cupcakes. How do you say no to a birthday girl? So we headed toward the bakery and picked up the cupcakes. As I was distracted by a clearance shelf, Noah was busy standing up in the cart, excitedly waving and joyfully proclaiming, "Hi, old person! It's my birthday to-day!"

Before I could calm her, he stopped and turned to her. His expression softened as he replied, "Well, hello, little lady! Happy birthday!"They chatted for a few minutes. Then, Noah turned to me and asked, "Can I take a picture with him?"I told her we'd certainly ask. I approached him and asked if he'd take a photo with my daughter for her birthday. His expression changed from confused to stunned to delighted. "A photo? With me?" he asked. "Yes, sure, for my birthday!"Noah answered. And so he did. I pulled out my iPhone, and they posed together. She placed her soft hand on top of his. He wordlessly stared at her with twinkling eyes as she kept his hand in hers, kissed the top of his hand and then placed it on her cheek. They were chatting like long-lost friends. I asked his name, and he told us to call him Dan. We were blocking other shoppers, but they didn't care. There was magic happening in the grocery store that day, and we could all feel it.

注意：

1. 续写词数应为 150 左右

2. 请按如下格式在答题卡的相应位置作答

After a few minutes, I thanked Mr. Dan for spending a bit of his day with us.

A few days later, we visited Mr. Dan's tidy house.

三、文本故事架构

本文属于"人与社会"——"良好的人际关系与社会交往"主题语境。主要讲述的是作者——"我"的小女儿在她四岁生日的当天，在面包店偶遇一位老人，并和老人成为朋友，温暖孤独老人的动人故事。考生在阅读这类文本时，应把握故事发展的三条线，即时空线、故事情节线和情感发展线。

(一)时空线

故事发生的地点在面包店和老人的家。

The day before my daughter Noah's fourth birthday…→The following day 等。

(二)故事情节线

Noah 向来对老人有一种特殊的关爱。在她四岁生日的当天,在面包店遇到了一位老人 Dan,Noah 热情地和老人打招呼,主动分享生日的喜悦,并和老人合照。Dan 被 Noah 真诚热情打动,成为好友,Noah 的出现也逐渐改变了他的生活。

(三)情感发展线

女儿 Noah 关爱老年人群体(同情)→遇见老人 Dan 合影(热情)→在此期间,老人的情感:迷惑→惊讶→开心。本文的标题"Love Will Melt Your Heart"有多重含义:一方面指的是四岁的小女孩 Noah 对于 Dan 的关心和爱最终融化了老人的心。从另一方面来说,文中的作者"我"作为旁观者也被女儿和老人之间的爱所感染,深受感动,爱也融化了"我"的心。

四、关键信息梳理

(一)人物

语篇出现了 3 个人物,"我"、女孩 Noah 和老人 Dan,都是关键人物。

文本中的关键词有:Noah,Dan,love,girl,excitedly,photo,magic 等。这些词汇在续写情节的发展和形成过程中,起着非常重要的作用。Noah 和 Dan 是本文主人公,love 是本文中的情感主线。

(二)提示句分析

根据第一段提示句"After a few minutes,I thanked Mr. Dan for spending a bit of his day with us"我们可以推断出,当"我"感谢老人的同时,老人亦对女儿 Noah 充满感谢,是 Noah 的快乐感染了他,让他度过了一段难忘的快乐时光。那么老人原本的生活为何失意呢? 或许是因为妻子的离世。

根据第二段提示句"A few days later,we visited Mr. Dan's tidy house"我们可以推断出,第一段的结尾处应合理铺垫"我"是如何联系上老人并且得知老人的住址的。之后"我"带着女儿 Noah 去拜访老人,可设想老人屋里的陈设是什么样的,而 Noah 又说了什么,做了什么,逐渐治愈了老人的心灵。那么此时,作为父亲的"我"又感悟到了什么呢?

五、写作思路构建

我感谢老人愿意花时间陪女儿 Noah 闲聊,而老人告诉我,Noah 才是那个他要感谢的人,他已经好久没有这么开心过了。我深受感动,把和老人的合影以及他们的故事发布在自己的脸书上。有位知情人士告诉我,老人的妻子几个月前刚离世。我询问了老人的联系方式以及住址,带着女儿 Noah 去拜访老人,并在老人的家中度过了愉快的时光。Noah 和老人依旧交谈甚欢,像认识多年的好友。Noah 时常牵挂老人,老人也总挂念 Noah。最近一次拜访老人时,他告诉我,自从遇见 Noah 后,他每晚都睡得很香,是 Noah 治愈了他,我湿了眼眶。

(一)习作欣赏

After a few minutes, I thanked Mr. Dan for spending a bit of his day with us. With tears in his eyes, he said, "No, thank you. This is the best day I've ever had in a long time." With a kind and good-humored spirit, he turned to my daughter. "Look! How much pleasure you've brought to me, Miss Noah." They gave each other a loving hug and Noah watched him until he was out of view. I was blown away by this meeting and posted the story and a photo on my Face book. Later that night, I received a private message, from which I learned that Mr. Dan's wife, Mary, had passed away six months earlier, and he had been lonely and depressed since then. I asked for Mr. Dan's phone number and planned to pay a visit someday.

A few days later, we visited Mr. Dan's tidy house. We spent nearly three hours with him that day. He was patient and kind with my talkative, constantly moving girl. Actually after the visit, Noah was still concerned about Mr. Dan, everyday asking about his health and hoping that he could feel loved. So was Mr. Dan. During another recent visit, he told me that he had slept soundly every night since meeting my girl. "Noah has healed me," he said. That left me speechless and my cheeks wet with tears. Seventy eight years separate these two people in age. Somehow, their hearts and souls seem to have recognized each other from long ago.

(二)习作评价

女孩 Noah 的父亲和老人 Dan 充满感动。老人流泪感谢父女俩陪他度过的快乐时光;而当他感谢小女孩 Noah 时,老人是和蔼愉悦的。这些描写使老人的形象丰满起来了。故事的结尾处,小女孩的父亲感动地流下了眼泪,这进一步凸显了文章的主题:爱会融化人的心。

第三节　后悔内疚

当一个人面对已经发生的做错的事情,或者是不完美的事情时,常会有产生后悔、内疚之情。这是一种必要的情绪反应,后悔内疚能使人明晰过往,启迪未来。这种情绪是读后续写中"人与自我"主题语境常考的考点。

一、构建语料库

(一)词汇短语

1. 单词

guilty	adj. 内疚的;惭愧的;有罪的	regretfully	adv. 遗憾地;痛惜地;失望地;懊悔地
regret	n. & v. 遗憾;后悔	shame	n. 羞耻(心);羞愧(感);可耻的事或人;
regretful	adj. 后悔的;失望的;令人惋惜的;遗憾的		

2. 词组

feel guilty about/at	因为……感到内疚
have regrets about doing sth.	对做某事有遗憾
it is a shame to do sth…	是个遗憾/可耻的
put…to shame	使感到羞耻;使丢脸
regret doing sth.	后悔做了某事
egret+that/wh-从句	后悔……
regret to say/tell/inform that	很遗憾地说/告诉/通知
to sb's regret	让某人遗憾的是
to sb's shame	令某人感到羞愧的是

(二)话题情景

①I felt incredibly ashamed of myself. 我自己感到无比羞愧。

②I now regret saying what I said. 我后悔刚才我说的话。

③"I should like to go with you very much,"replied Susan,with a sigh.

Susan 叹了口气,说:"我很愿意跟你们一块去。"

④I stood there,with regretful tears in my eyes.

我站在那儿,眼里含着后悔的泪水。

⑤If only she had not left her mobile phone in that bag with Tom.

要是没有把手机落在 Tom 的包里就好了!

⑥Thinking about what I had done to him,regret and guilt overwhelmed me like endless tides.

一想到我对他所做的一切,遗憾和内疚就像没休止的潮水一样向我袭来。

(三)情景语段

"Why? why there is no meal,mom?"I uttered an impatient complaint at the sight of the empty table. "I just came back from work,dear. "Hearing mom's tired voice,I was immediately ruled by a flood of guilty. With my head down,I stepped toward mom in an incredible shame,making a true apology. Mom smiled and patted me on the shoulder,showing her forgiveness.

I realized how rude my behaviour was!

二、语篇分析

2016 年浙江省高考题

阅读下面材料,根据其内容和所给段落开头语续写两段,使之构成一篇完整的短文。

One weekend in July,Jane and her husband,Tom,had driven three hours to camp overnight by a lake in the forest. Unfortunately,on the way an unpleasant subject came up and they started to quarrel. By the time they reached the lake, Jane was so angry that she said to Tom. "I'm going to find a better spot for us to camp"and walked away.

With no path to follow,Jane just walked on for quite a long time. After she had climbed to a high place,she turned around,hoping to see the lake. To her surprise,she saw nothing but forest and,far beyond,a snow capped mountain top. She suddenly realized that she was lost.

"Tom!"she cried. "Help!"

No reply. If only she had not left her mobile phone in that bag with Tom. Jane kept moving,but the farther she walked,the more confused she became. As night was beginning to fall, Jane was so tired that she had to stop for the night. Lying awake in the dark, Jane wanted very much to be with Tom and her family. She wanted to hold him and tell him how much she loved him.

Jane rose at the break of day, hungry and thirsty. She could hear water trickling（滴落）somewhere at a distance. Quickly she followed the sound to a stream. To her great joy, she also saw some berry bushes. She drank and ate a few berries. Never in her life had she tasted anything better. Feeling stronger now, Jane began to walk along the stream and hope it would lead her to the lake.

As she picked her way carefully along the stream, Jane heard a helicopter. Is that for me? Unfortunately, the trees made it impossible for people to see her from above. A few minutes later, another helicopter flew overhead. Jane took off her yellow blouse, thinking that she should go to an open area and flag them if they came back again.

注意：

1. 续写词数应为 150 左右

2. 请按如下格式在答题卡的相应位置作答

> But no more helicopters came and it was dark.
>
> It was daybreak when Jane woke up.

三、文本故事架构

本文属于"人与自我"——"做人与做事"主题语境。文章记叙了 Jane 与丈夫 Tom 驱车去森林野营，起初发生争吵，之后赌气离开，最后迷路的故事。在梳理故事情节发展的脉络时，我们要把握故事发展的三条线，即时空线、故事情节线和情感发展线。

（一）时空线

故事发生的地点依然是森林，被救出后可以回到家中。

one weekend in July→By the time they reached the lake→as night was beginning to fall→at the break of day→as she picked her way carefully along the stream→a few minutes later 等。

（二）故事情节线

Jane 与丈夫 Tom 去森林中的湖边野营，发生了争吵，Jane 独自进入森林后迷路，露宿一宿，第二天仅以溪水野果为食，并沿溪前行。有直升机飞过，Jane 准备以黄色衬衣吸引直升机注意。

（三）情感发展线

夫妻两人闹情绪,Jane 的情感发展经历了以下变化:Jane 与丈夫吵架后独自进入森林(生气)→意识到自己迷路了(恐惧)→反思行为(后悔)→躺在黑暗中(思念丈夫)→直升机经过(充满希望)→直升机飞走(遗憾)。

四、关键信息梳理

（一）人物

语篇中只有两个人物,Jane 和 Tom,因此续写的主角是他们。

文本中的关键词是 Jane,Tom,walked,climbed,stream,to her great joy,helicopter,yellow blouse 等。这些词是设计情节的基础。Jane 是故事的核心人物,helicopter 和 yellow blouse 是获救的重要线索。故事发生在野外,stream,walked 和 climbed 这三个词都可以参考。

（二）提示句分析

根据第一段首句"But no more helicopter came and it was getting dark again"的提示,我们可以推断出,Jane 在森林里又待了一个夜晚,根据前文的文本,我们围绕 Jane 的所见、所闻和所想展开,在这一过程中,她的内心是害怕的、后悔的,同时对丈夫又有着非常强烈的思念的心理。因此,续写的第一段应该将 Jane 的心理活动和环境写出来。

根据第二段首句"It was daybreak when Jane woke up"的提示,我们可以推断出,Jane 醒来了,被营救了和丈夫 Tom 团圆,意识到自己行为的鲁莽,更加珍惜彼此的感情。

五、写作思路构建

思路一:夜晚来临,Jane 感到害怕,思念丈夫,但求生最关键,于是找到一个安全的地方先睡一觉。第二天她醒来在空地上耐心等候,听到直升机的声音后使劲挥舞着黄衬衫成功引起注意,接着丈夫从直升机里出来,夫妻团圆。

思路二:Jane 在森林里又度过了一个晚上。她利用火柴点燃树枝给自己保暖,疲惫中不知不觉入睡。第二天醒来,Jane 一路沿着小溪走,来到一个湖,幸运地碰到了两个警察,他们正在寻找她,原来是 Tom 报了警。在警察的带路下,Jane 和 Tom 最后夫妻团聚。

（一）习作欣赏

<u>But no more helicopters came and it was dark.</u> There was nothing but silence. Jane was extremely frightened and missed her husband, Tom, a great

deal. She couldn't help crying, clutching her hair. However, having a deep breath, Jane concentrated all efforts on walking down along the stream. To her great joy, she eventually reached an open area. Feeling exhausted, she fell asleep.

It was daybreak when Jane woke up. The sun shone lightly, bringing warmth and hope to the world. Jane stayed at the open area patiently to wait for others' help. Two hours later, the helicopter which she had seen yesterday caught her eyes. Jane took off her yellow blouse to flag them and yelled out to make the helicopter notice her. Fortunately, the helicopter noticed her and came closer, finally landing at the open area. Her husband, Tom, got out of the helicopter. Surprised and overjoyed a great deal, Jane held him tightly and told him how much she loved him. At the moment, the mountain was filled with love.

(二)习作评价

文章以情感发展为线索,从害怕、后悔、不安,到得救后的喜悦。正是有了前文迷路后的沮丧与恐惧才能凸显得救后的喜悦和激动。通过动作描写体现出 Jane 的后悔之意,直接的形容词描写体现了她的不自在,最后非谓语动词和动作描写的运用让我们真切地感受到她得救后的喜悦。

第四节　惊慌恐惧

惊慌、恐惧是指在危险中或者陌生的环境中,感受到的一种强烈而压抑的情感状态,表现为:神经紧张,内心充满害怕,无法集中注意力,脑子里一片空白,求生、求安全的心理强烈。读后续写试题中有很多关于这种心理活动的命题。

一、构建语料库

(一)词汇短语

1. 单词

fear	n. 害怕;恐惧 v. 害怕;畏惧	scream	v. & n. 尖叫着;尖叫声;刺耳声音
frighten	v. (使)惊恐;(使)惊吓	terrible	adj. 可怕的;令人不快的
frightened	adj. 受惊的;害怕的	terrified	adj. 非常害怕的;极度惊恐的
panic	n. 恐慌;惊慌 v. (使)恐慌	terrify	v. 使恐惧;恐吓
scare	v. 使恐惧;使害怕	terror	n. 惊恐;恐怖;引起恐怖的人/物

2. 词组

be frightened of	害怕(做)某事
be in a state of panic	陷入惊慌
(be) scared of (doing) sth.	害怕(做)某事
(be) scared to do sth.	害怕做某事
(be) scared to death	害怕得要死
choke with fear	因害怕而哽咽
fear to do/doing sth.	害怕做某事
for fear of /for fear (that)	生怕;以免
get into a panic	陷入惊慌
in panic	害怕地
scream in/with fear	吓得尖叫
tremble from head to toe	全身颤抖
turn pale	脸色变苍白

(二)话题情景

①A flood of fear welled up in him. 他从心底害怕。

②That horror movie made my hair stand on end.

那部恐怖电影使我的头发竖起来。

③She shook all over, feeling like sitting on pins and needles.

她浑身发抖,如坐针毡。

④A snake came out of the brushwood and scared me to death.

一条蛇从灌木丛爬出来,把我吓坏了。

⑤My heart stood still when I saw the little baby was to fall from the second floor.

当我看到小婴儿要从二楼摔下来时,我怔住了。

⑥Last night, I dreamed about being chased by an angry dog. I really had my heart in my mouth.

昨晚,我梦见被一只恶狗追赶,我真的被吓坏了。

(三)情景语段

I was sleeping when the fire broke out. Choked by the smog flooding in, I coughed a lot, which woke me up in a terrible way. Seeing the increasingly thick smog dancing crazily, I was deeply seized by great fear. With my mind racing, I forced myself to recall and follow those secure tips learned before, including putting a piece of wet cloth against my nose and bowing to escape, though already scared to death. Much fortunately, I managed to survive the disaster. Completely consumed by the tiredness, I let out a sign of relief.

二、语篇分析

2018 年浙江高考试题

阅读下面材料, 根据其内容和所给段落开头语续写两段, 使之构成一篇完整的短文。

It was summer, and my dad wanted to treat me to a vacation like never before. He decided to take me on a trip to the Wild West.

We took a plane to Albuquerque, a big city in the state of New Mexico. We reached Albuquerque in the late afternoon. Uncle Paul, my dad's friend, picked us up from the airport and drove us up to his farm in Pecos.

His wife Tina cooked us a delicious dinner and we got to know his sons Ryan and Kyle. My dad and I spent the night in the guestroom of the farm house listening to the frogs and water rolling down the river nearby. Very early in the morning, Uncle Paul woke us up to have breakfast. "The day starts at dawn on my farm," he said. After breakfast, I went to help Aunt Tina feed the chickens. while my dad went with Uncle Paul to take the sheep out to graze(吃草). I was impressed to see my dad and Uncle Paul riding horses. They looked really cool.

In the afternoon, I asked Uncle Paul if I could take a horse ride, and he said yes, as long as my dad went with me. I wasn't going to take a horse ride by myself anyway. So, my dad and I put on our new cowboy hats, got on our horses, and headed slowly towards the mountains. "Don't be late for supper," Uncle Paul cried, "and keep to the track so that you don't get lost!" "OK!" my dad cried back. After a while Uncle Paul and his farm house were out of sight. It was so peaceful and quiet and the colors of the brown rocks, the deep green pine trees, and the late afternoon sun mixed to create a magic scene. It looked like a beautiful woven(编织的)blanket spread out upon the ground just for us.

注意:

1. 续写词数应为 150 左右

2. 请按如下格式在答题卡的相应位置作答

> Suddenly a little rabbit jumped out in front of my horse.
> We had no idea where we were and it was getting dark.

三、文本故事架构

本文属于"人与自我"——"生活与学习"主题语境。文章主要记叙了父亲为了让"我"过一个不同以往的暑假,带"我"去了 Uncle Paul 的农场。在那里,"我"在父亲的陪伴下,体验了一次骑马历险的经历。考生在阅读这类文本时,应把握故事发展的三条线,即时空线、故事情节线和情感发展线。

(一)时空线

从 New Mexico 出发,先到 Albuquerque 机场,后到叔叔家农场。

(background) one summer day…→(the first day) in the late afternoon,…→spent the night…→(the second day) very early in the morning…→after the breakfast…→in the afternoon…→after a while…等。

(二)故事情节线

父亲带我去西部荒野的一个朋友 Uncle Paul 家的农场,让我过一个不一样的假期。第一天,下午叔叔到机场接我们,晚上在农场听青蛙叫和潺潺的水声。第二天,一早吃过早饭,体验了农场的生活。见爸爸和叔叔骑马,我很好奇,也想骑马,于是亲身上马,爸爸也和我一起体验骑马。出发前,叔叔叮嘱我们要沿着足迹走并在晚饭前赶回来,不然会迷路。于是,我和父亲就出发了。

(三)情感发展线

爸爸要带我去西部让我度过一个不一样的假期(充满期待)→农场生活(新鲜好奇)→骑马前行(兴奋刺激)。

四、关键信息梳理

(一)人物

语篇出现了 6 个人物:"我"、dad、叔叔 Paul、叔叔的妻子 Tina、叔叔的儿子 Ryan 和 Kyle。但关键的人物是"我"、dad 和叔叔 Paul。

文本中的关键词有:dad, Uncle Paul, farmhouse, river, sheep, late, track, get lost, sight 等。这些关键词对故事情节的发展起着重要的作用。

"我"和 dad 是非常关键的角色。根据文本,Uncle Paul 在情节中反复出现,故事结局也要回到 Uncle Paul 的农场,因此他和 farmhouse 也是关键词汇。river 和 sheep 用于环境描写或者是帮助主人公回去的线索,因为前文提及农场附近是有河流的。track 在这篇文章里是关键的词,主人公偏离了原来的轨迹,才迷路了。get lost 是故事曲折的关键,是矛盾的核心,是必选要素。late 也很容易用到,因为迷路自然会 late for supper,或者天色渐晚。sight 这个词,也可能使用短语,如:catch sight sight/out of sight of/lose of/come into sight 等。

（二）提示句分析

根据第一段提示句"Suddenly a little rabbit jumped out in front of my horse"我们可以推断出,suddenly 表明情况发生了急剧变化。通过上文的景色描写,"我"和父亲正在欣赏沿途静谧优美的景色,这时突然蹦出一只兔子,肯定会打破原有的平静。本段主要写马、"我"以及父亲的反应和心理活动发生的相应变化。

根据第二段提示句"We had no idea where we were and it got dark"我们可以推断出,"我们"迷路了,说明上文中"我们"因为兔子的出现而偏离了原来的轨迹。可能是追着兔子不知不觉跑远了,也可能是马儿受到惊吓带着"我"乱跑导致迷路,但故事的结局是,"我们"最终还是回到了农场。因此,本段主要是描写如何回农场了。语言的重点更要放在人物在天黑迷路时的心理活动、环境描写以及父亲行为等的刻画上。

五、写作思路构建

兔子突然出现,吸引了我,我骑马跟着,欣赏沿途美丽景色并沉醉其中,最后渐渐偏离了来时的路。

我们都不确定自己到底走到了哪里,而这时候天色已晚。因为环境陌生,我和父亲都不敢贸然行动,生怕越走越远,碰到更大的危险,只得待在原地,期待叔叔能来找我们。等了一段时间,果然叔叔拿着火炬,呼叫着我和父亲的名字。最后,在叔叔的带领下,我们回到了农场。

无论哪个思路,续写部分的最后应和文章开头吻合在一起:爸爸让我享受了一个从没有过的假期:充满刺激,体验了快乐。

（一）习作欣赏

Suddenly a little rabbit jumped out in front of my horse. "What a lovely rabbit!" I shouted with terrific excitement. "Dad, let's catch it as our pet!" I suggested. Entirely forgetting what Uncle Paul had told us, we chased after that pretty rabbit. Unfortunately, so clever and swift was it that it disappeared in the forest before long. Not until then did we realize that the last ray of twilight was quickly disappearing among the numerous trees and we couldn't find our track at all! We did get lost.

　　We had no idea where we were and it was getting dark. "Dad, what can we do?" I threw my arms around him tightly, seized by a start of horror. Dad comforted me in a gentle voice. We wandered in the scary forest and didn't know what horrible things would happen to us, hoping to find the way back. Suddenly, we heard the sound of water rolling down the river. We decided to follow the river. After a while, we heard the familiar sound of sheep and then caught sight of the farmhouse. The family were waiting for us in the distance, Seeing this, smiles lit up both of our faces.

（二）习作评价

　　时间的流逝和黑夜的到来,推动了故事情节的发展,与下文的 getting dark 衔接;scary,horrible 词的运用以及比喻修辞的运用,渲染了紧张的气氛,也烘托了主人公内心的害怕、恐惧;同时,河流和羊的声音也为故事的结局提供了线索和出路,给故事画上了圆满的句号。

第五节　生气愤怒

　　生气、愤怒的心理特征是读后续写试题中常见的考点。这种心理活动常常和身体语言描写相结合,如果再恰当地增加直接引语,就会生动形象地刻画出生气、愤怒的画面。

一、构建语料库

（一）词汇短语

1. 单词

anger	n. 生气;愤怒　v. 激怒	aggressively	adv. 攻击地;有闯劲地;激烈地
angry	adj. 发怒的;生气的	breathless	adj. 气喘吁吁的,喘不过气来的
annoy	v. 使恼怒;使烦恼	hot-tempered	adj. 性情暴躁的
annoyed	adj. 恼怒的;烦恼的	mad	adj. 恼火的;发疯的

2. 词组

arouse one's displeasure	引起不愉快
a look of burning anger glared at sb	怒视某人
(be) angry at/with sb.	生某人的气
(be) angry about/at/over sth.	因为某事生气
be easily annoyed at	易于生气
be seized by anger	暴怒
complain constantly about sth.	不断抱怨
could hardly/scarcely contain his rage	不能控制怒火
explode with anger	勃然大怒
get mad/cross at sb.	勃然大怒
in anger	生气地
ignore a complaint	不理抱怨
run out of the room in a burst of anger	一阵恼怒跑出房间
stamp one's feet in anger	气得跺脚
tremble with anger	气得颤抖

(二)话题情景

①Anger nearly consumed her. 愤怒几乎吞噬了她。

②Anger welled up in his chest. 愤怒涌上他的心头。

③She was breathless with anger. 她气得喘不过气来。

④Anger rose in him like a tide. 愤怒像潮水般涌上心头。

⑤Anger rushed/poured through her. 愤怒从她身上涌了出来。

⑥Boiling with anger,Tom shook his fist at me.

怒火心中烧,Tom 朝我挥舞拳头。

⑦Tom felt so angry that he stormed out of the room,shutting the door hard behind him.

Tom 冲出房间,狠狠地摔门而去。

(三)情景语段

Seeing my handwriting making no progress my English teacher could hardly contain his deep disappointment and rage. With his eyes cooler and cooler,I knew anger was rising wildly in him like a tide. I was waiting for a storm. However,to my surprise and relief, though consumed by anger, he still corrected my silly mistakes with enormous patience, which moved me a lot.

二、语篇分析

阅读下面短文,根据内容和所给段落开头语续写两段,使之构成一个完整的短文。

I have kept a watch from my grandfather's, though the glass face is broken.

When I was schoolboy, the watch hung by my grandfather's bed. The face was marked with elegant Roman numerals. It was a magnificent watch and I often gazed at it longingly sitting with my grandfather after school. He would often ask about my progress at school. The day I told him of my success in the examinations, he was overcome with pleasure. "You'll be going to the new school next. And then you'll go to university, Will?" he asked. "But you'll need plenty of patience. Patience and hard work. That's the way to succeed."

He took off the watch, wound it and gazed at it. "It was given me for fifty years of faithful service with my firm," he said proudly. Finally, he handed me the watch as the progress in school. I held it, feeling its weight.

As I was leaving him, he said, "And you'll not forget what I told you?"

"No, granddad," I promised, "I'll not."

Arriving home, my mother was to hold it in trust until she considered me old enough to look after it, but I protested strongly that she finally agreed to hang it where I could always see it.

The summer ended and it was time for me to enter the new school. I had never made friends easily there. One boy, Crawley, was a well-to-do fellow whose way of impressing us was toparade(炫耀) his possessions. His bicycle was new, everything, in fact, was better than ours—until he brought a watch. Crawley said his watch was absolutely the finest watch.

"I have a better watch," I announced.

"Well, show it to us," Crawley said sneeringly(轻蔑地).

"I'll bring it this afternoon," I said. "Then you'll see."

I rode my bike home, wondering how I would persuade my mother to let me take the watch. Luckily, she stepped outside and I slipped the watch into my pocket. I rode my bike fast to school, excitement through me.

注意:

1. 续写词数应为 150 左右

2.请按如下格式在答题卡的相应位置作答

> *Suddenly I fell over heavily to the ground due to the very rough road. When I said my mothercould't let me bring the watch, they burst into laughter.*

三、文本故事架构

本文属于"人与自我"——"做人与做事"主题语境。因为"我"学习成绩得到了祖父的认可,他把非常珍贵的手表传给"我",并要求"我"耐心、刻苦。得知"我"有只非凡的表,同学要"我"拿到学校来看看,回家取了表,"我"兴奋地向学校走去。考生在阅读这类文本时,应把握故事发展的三条线,即时空线、故事情节线和情感发展线。

(一)时空线

故事发生在家中,学校途中以及学校里。

When a schoolboy…→As leaving him,…→Arriving home,mother…→The summer… enter the new school→Crawley … showed off …→I rode my bike home 等。

(二)故事情节线

因为我学习成绩得到了祖父的认可,他把非常珍贵的手表传给我。他要求我耐心、刻苦。妈妈把这只表挂在家里显眼的位置。得知我有只非凡的表,同学要我拿出来看看,回家取了表,兴奋地向学校走去。

(三)情感发展线

我学习成绩优秀,祖父把珍贵的表传给我,并要求我耐心、刻苦(殷切希望)→妈妈托管表(抗议)→进入新学校,同学 Crawley 爱炫耀,我回家取表(急切)。

四、关键信息梳理

(一)人物

语篇出现了 4 个人物,但关键的是"我"、妈妈和 Crawley。

文本中的关键词有:the watch, mother, Crawley, laughing, grandfather's words 等。这些词汇在续写情节的形成和发展过程中,起着非常重要的作用,抓住了这些关键词就抓住了续写的思路。

(二)提示句分析

根据第一段提示句"*Suddenly I fell over heavily to the ground due to the* very rough road"我们可以推断出,"我"回家拿出表后,在去学校路上发生的故事,侧重心理描写。而且根据第二句提示句,作者没有把表展示给同学看,表可能摔坏了或者丢了。

根据第二段提示句"When I said my mother couldn't let me bring the watch,they burst into laughter"我们可以推断出,主要是写"我"拿不出表的借口,同学们,特别是 Crawley 的嘲弄,以及"我"的感悟。

五、写作思路构建

因为道路特别崎岖,我骑车不稳,重重地摔在地上。我一步也不能挪,我挣扎着站起来,把手伸到口袋里,拿出了祖父最骄傲的表。看到表盘玻璃碎了,我愣愣地僵住了。回到学校,当我跟同学们说,妈妈不让我把表拿到学校来的时候,他们立即大笑起来"你编得多好的故事啊!"Crawley 轻蔑地回应,别的同学也跟着喊叫起来。我非常愤怒,气得快哭了。我静静地坐在桌子边,回想着祖父给我表时的话。我突然间明白我辜负了祖父的期望:做事一定要有耐心,学习一定要刻苦。

(一)习作欣赏

Suddenly I fell over heavily to the ground due to the very rough road. My hands hurt so much that I could not move an inch! After I managed to pick myself up slowly, I put a trembling hand into my pocket and brought out what was left of my grandfather's proudest possession with care. I froze there seeing the glass was broken, and the Roman numerals looked crazily at one another. I put the watch back and rode slowly on to school, numb with misery.

When I said my mother couldn't let me bring the watch, they burst into laughter. "What a story!" Crawley said sneeringly. The others took up his cries. Anger welled up in my chest. I nearly wept, for it was the saddest moment of my young life. As I sat quietly at my desk, a strange feeling stole over me. It was not shame at my classmates' laughing, nor was it fear of my mother's anger. All I could think of was my grandfather's words, "Patience, Will, patience." The broken watch I keep is a good reminder. Since then, I have learned to be more patient and to work harder. I live up to grandfather's wishes.

(二)习作评价

续写部分用词较为地道,情节融洽度高。取表回校途中的情绪变化大,由激动变成了沮丧和痛苦。到校后同学的嘲笑,特别是 Crawley 的得意洋洋,作者的愤怒之情溢于言表。文末,作者想起了祖父的话,照应了全文。

第六节　同情怜悯

当别人遇到情感的忧伤,情绪的低落或运气不佳时,需要我们用恰当的方式对对方表达同情和怜悯,表示安慰和提供帮助。

一、构建语料库

(一)词汇短语

1.单词

awkward	adj. 尴尬的;别扭的;使用不便的	mercy	n. 仁慈;怜悯;恩惠;宽恕
embarrass	v. 使窘迫;使尴尬	pity	n. & v. 同情;怜悯
embarrassed	adj. 尴尬的	sympathy	n. 同情(心)
embarrassing	adj. 令人尴尬的		

2.词组

accept sb's sympathy	接受某人的慰问
at the mercy of	任……摆布,在……前毫无办法
be embarrassed about	因为……感到尴尬
beyond one's expectations	出乎某人意料地
express sympathy	表示慰问
feel sorry for	同情……
feel sympathy for	同情……
it was a pity (that)…	很遗憾……
let sb. down	使失望;辜负
take pity on sb.	同情某人
out ofsympathy	出于同情
without mercy	无情地

(二)话题情景

①She pressed my hand in sympathy. 她同情地紧紧握住我的手。

②Place accept my heart felt you're welcome. 请接受我诚挚的慰问。

③I'm sorry to learn about the accident. 获悉此次事故,我深感悲伤。

④Let me convey my deepest sympathy to you.

允许我向您表示最深切的同情。

⑤I regret to tell you that the school meeting has been canceled due to the COVID-19.

因为新冠疫情的原因,我遗憾地告诉大家校运会已经取消。

（三）情景语段

Suffering from the failure of high jump at his second attempt, John collapsed to the ground, torn by sadness. A strong flood of sympathy welled up in my mind. Unable to bear his lack of hope, I paced towards him, patted him on the shoulder softly and conveyed my heart felt comfort and encouragement.

二、语篇分析

阅读下面短文,根据内容和所给段落开头语续写两段,使之构成一个完整的短文。

Adventure with a Cuckoo

Not far from our house in Texas was a thick woodland. There I spent much of my time. I was an animal-lover, eager to watch—and capture, if possible—the interesting creatures that lived there.

Walking one afternoon in the depths of the woodland, I came upon a huge hollow（空的）log. I looked cautiously into it, and to my excitement, there was the figure of a cuckoo（杜鹃鸟）. It was probably a mother bird sitting on her eggs. Eagerly I dragged two large stones to one end of the log and closed the opening there.

If I wanted the bird, I would have to go get her. The log was almost twenty feet long. Could I get through it? Would the cuckoo peck（啄）at me?

In spite of my fears, I started in. I inched forward with my arms stretched out in front of me and my toes digging into the earth. My face was pressed against the wet wood. I could not bring my arms back, because there was not enough room.

Suddenly I realized that the cuckoo and I were not the only things in the hollow log. I trembled. What was this soft thing my hand felt? It was the nest of white-footed mice! The bright-eyed little creatures bounced for the darkest places they could find in a panic. They raced over my back, under my shirt, about my neck. One of them crawled between my body and the wood! I gave a wild shrug. Many other creatures, like insects were on the run for a safe place. Poor harmless little creatures! How guilty I was to have disturbed their life!

Suddenly I saw the mother cuckoo stood up, hissed(斯叫), and coughed. I wished that I hadn't covered up the other end of the log. I drove off the great bird. She hissed forward painfully.

Then I was face to face with a lovely newborn baby cuckoo. It was downy white, with gray legs and naked head. Breathing quietly, it rested in the nest.

注意:

1. 续写词数应为 150 左右

2. 请按如下格式在答题卡的相应位置作答

I wormed my way ahead carefully with the baby bird in my hand.

I had planned to take the mother and the baby cuckoo home.

三、文本故事架构

本文属于"人与自然"——"人与动物"主题语境。"我"喜欢鸟,在家附近的小树林里的原木中发现了杜鹃鸟以及新生的杜鹃鸟宝宝。"我"手里捧着杜鹃鸟宝宝,前面赶着杜鹃鸟妈妈,历经困难爬出了原木。考生在阅读这类文本时,应把握故事发展的三条线,即时空线、故事情节线和情感发展线。

(一)时空线

故事发生在家附近的小树林里 20 米长的原木中。

one afternoon entered...→in the log...→out of the log 等。

(二)故事情节线

我非常喜欢鸟,有时间我就去我家附近的小树林去看鸟。有一个下午,我在树林中看到了一个中间空空的原木,有 20 多米长。我好奇地朝里看,非常兴奋的是,原木里边有只杜鹃鸟! 尽管很害怕,我仍继续向前。进入原木,我发现除了杜鹃鸟,里面还有老鼠,以及各种各样的昆虫,纠缠着我,我害怕得很,挣扎着爬行,很多昆虫在周围,我很内疚,打扰了他们的生活。突然间,我看到这只杜鹃鸟妈妈痛苦地嘶叫着前行,我又突然发现一只新生的杜鹃鸟宝宝。

(三)情感发展线

发现原木中有杜鹃鸟(非常兴奋)→继续前行,遇到老鼠以及各种昆虫(后悔内疚)→见杜鹃鸟撕裂痛苦地叫着和新初生的杜鹃鸟宝宝(同情)。

四、关键信息梳理

(一)人物

语篇出现的人物较少,只有"我"和杜鹃鸟,以及杜鹃鸟宝宝。

文本中的关键词有:cuckoo,newborn baby cuckoo,stones,the hollow log,hissed,painfully 和 guilty 等。这些词汇在续写情节的形成和发展过程中,起着非常重要的作用。抓住了这些关键词就抓住了续写的思路。

(二)提示句分析

根据第一段提示句"I wormed my way ahead carefully with the baby bird in my hand"我们可以推断出,这一段主要是写从原木中爬出来的艰难经过以及心理活动。

根据第二段提示句"I had planned to take the mother and the baby cuckoo home"我们可以推断出,这一段主要是写走出原木以后,"我"看到杜鹃鸟和杜鹃鸟宝宝痛苦的情况,决定将其放归自然的过程以及杜鹃鸟回家后的情况。

五、写作思路构建

我手中托着杜鹃鸟宝宝,小心翼翼地向前爬行。原木空间狭小,老鼠和各种各样的昆虫,烦扰着我,我非常非常地害怕。等到我爬出原木,我欣慰地喘了口气。我原是想把这只杜鹃鸟和杜鹃鸟宝宝带回家的,但是我又不忍心让杜鹃鸟因离开家园而痛苦,出于同情,我又把杜鹃鸟和宝宝放在了原木中。回家以后妈妈问我为什么回家晚了,我把事情的经过说给她听,妈妈表扬我做的对。

(一)习作欣赏

I wormed my way ahead carefully with the baby bird in my hand. The parent bird drew back. At the end of the log I grabbed her by the feet. How pleased I was to catch bird in the log! Probably my parents would be proud, too. I pushed the stones away and breathed fresh air in deep gasps. Nearly worn out, I trembled from head to foot. It took me great pains to climb out. In the bright light, mother and baby showed greater panic and uneasiness.

I had planned to take the mother and the baby cuckoo home. However, I couldn't bring myself to take the baby away or leave it there an orphan. The baby's painful eyes seemed to beg me to spare her. Sympathetically I put baby back in the hollow log and put the mother beside it. I flicked the dust off my clothes and smoothed back my hair and then headed home. When I reached home, my mother was waiting for me. She asked me why I was so late, I told mother what had happened. Hearing my story, she said in an appreciative tone, "You are right, my son. Mother is inseparable from children!"

(二)习作评价

续写故事写得非常生动,情节设计得也非常好,特别是文本塑造的这个小男孩的性格,是爱鸟护鸟的角色,所以当爬出原木以后,看到杜鹃鸟痛苦的情况,出于同情,又把杜鹃鸟和杜鹃鸟宝宝放回到原木中。"The babies painful eyes seemed to beg me to spare him"拟人化的写法非常得体。

第七节　兴趣爱好

构建资料库

(一)词汇短语

1.单词

attract	v.吸引;引起(……的兴趣)	fan	n.(运动、电影等的)狂热爱好者;迷
attraction	n.吸引(力);有吸引力的事/人	favor	n.好感;赞同;恩惠 v.喜爱;支持
curiosity	n.好奇心	favorite	adj.最喜爱的 n.心爱的人/物
eager	adj.渴望的;热切的	fun	n.享乐;乐趣
engage	n.吸引;(使)参加;(使)参与;聘请	hobby	n.业余爱好
enjoyable	adj.令人愉快的;有乐趣的	intense	adj.强大的;强烈的;热情的
enrich	v.使富裕;丰富	interest	n.兴趣;爱好 v.使……感兴趣
entertain-ment	n.娱乐;娱乐节目/活动	magic	n.魔法;魔术;魅力 adj.魔法的;不可思议的
enthusiasm	n.热情;热忱	pastime	n.消遣;娱乐
enthusiastic	adj.(充满)热情的;热心的	pursue	v.追求;(继续)从事;追赶
explore	v.探测;探讨;探究	recreation	n.消遣;娱乐

2. 词组

appeal to	对……有吸引力
be eager to do sth.	渴望做某事
be eager for	渴望……
be crazy/mad about	对……着迷;热衷于
be enthusiastic about	对(做)某事充满了热情
be fond of	对……喜欢
be(of)benefit to	对……有益
be of no interest	毫无兴趣
be struck by/with	被迷住
for fun	为了玩乐
for sb's benefit/for the benefit of sb.	为了某人(的利益)
have fun	作乐;玩乐
have/develop an interest in	对……产生兴趣
have a gift for...	有天赋
in favour of	赞同;支持
lack/be full of enthusiasm	缺乏/充满热情
make fun of	取笑;拿……开玩笑
out of curiosity	出于好奇
satisfy/arouse sb's curiosity	满足/激起某人的好奇心
show/lose interest in	对……表现出/失去兴趣
show off	卖弄;炫耀
take up	开始(从事);占用
take one's eyes off...	把眼睛移开

(二)话题情景

①Taking good care of others is also my strength.
照顾好别人也是我的优点。
②We had great fun singing and dancing,telling jokes and stories.
我们从唱歌、跳舞、说笑话、讲故事中获得很多的乐趣。
③I know he's an intense player,but he does enjoy what he's doing.

我知道他是个拼命三郎,但他确实喜欢自己所做的事。

④It seems that the private lives of movie stars never fail to fascinate.

电影明星的私生活似乎总是使人津津乐道。

⑤School activities have not only enriched our school life but where prepared ourselves for developing their interests.

学校的各种活动不仅丰富了我们的校园生活,而且为培养其他兴趣奠定了基础。

(三)情景语段

English has become my interest. Every time I read it loudly, I felt myself held entirely by its unique charm. Enthusiastic about every English class, I practise my skills repeatedly and expect great progress. Diving myself in the deep sea of English, I have harvested a lot more than knowledge, which is worthy of my efforts.

二、语篇分析

阅读下面短文,根据内容和所给段落开头语续写两段,使之构成一个完整的短文。

Deep in the forest, my husband and I had fun climbing over and crawling under the downed trees that blocked the dirt path before us. It was May, yet we headed for a snow-covered hill. When we noticed our jeans were wet up to our knees, it did not dampen our spirits. Not once did we say, "Let's turn around." This was our vacation, and we were on an adventure. Little did we know this was the beginning of many more surprises.

The trail was marked as an easy one-kilometer hike, yet we were already walking a long distance. Our lightheartedness stopped when we came out into a clearing and saw a parking lot without our rental car in it. As my eyes scanned the surroundings, nothing looked familiar. My heart raced. I realized we were lost in a national park that did not officially open for another week.

Usually, I am the calm one in the relationship, but my husband surprised me with his calmness. This did not comfort me; in fact, it heightened my fear. As we walked, I asked my husband to call for help, but there was no cell-phone signal in this isolated (偏僻的) area.

It was awfully quiet except for our footsteps hitting the road, and my heavy breathing. My husband suggested we conserve energy and walk slower. With each step on the road, my feet and thighs hurt while my mind raced with thoughts about people who got lost in the Canadian woods for days.

My vision sharpened. I noticed everything around me: the trees, rocks and snow. I thought we could eat the snow on the ground in the event we needed water. For the first time in my life, I was ready and willing to get a ride, but we did not meet with a single car on the road. Silently, I prayed multiple times. We focused on each other, made joint decisions and connected through gratitude. We managed to stay on the main road and walked straight on.

注意:

1. 续写词数应为 150 左右

2. 请按如下格式在答题卡的相应位置作答

> My husband suddenly spotted a small building on a hill in the distance. Just then, a friendly woman appeared, saying, "Hello."

三、文本故事架构

本文属于"人与社会"——"体育与健康、体育精神"主题语境。主要讲了夫妻双方登山过程中遇到困难,最后在陌生女士的帮助下安全返回的故事。考生在阅读这类文本时,应把握故事发展的三条线,即时空线、故事情节线和情感发展线。

（一）时空线

故事发生在五月,国家公园森林深处,"我们"向有雪覆盖的山顶攀登的过程中。

（二）故事情节线

五月国家公园森林深处,我和丈夫兴致勃勃地向有雪覆盖的山顶攀登。开始的时候认为是很容易的爬山活动,但当我们走到空旷地带的时候,轻松的心情就没有了。周围的一切都不熟悉,我的心跳地更快了,我们在国家公园迷路了,没有手机信号,一切都非常的寂静,我和丈夫非常害怕。我们不断祈祷,保持在主路上前行。忽然,我们看到了远处有一栋建筑。

（三）情感发展线

五月国家公园森林深处,我和丈夫攀登有雪覆盖的山顶(兴致勃勃)→走到空旷地带的时候,周围的一切都不熟悉,在国家公园里迷路了(紧张)→没有手机信号,周围非常的寂静(害怕)→多次地祈祷,保持在主路上前行(坚定)→看到了远处有一栋建筑(欣慰)→和善的妇女出现在我们面前,跟我们热情打招呼(充满希望)。

四、关键信息梳理

(一)人物

语篇出现了 3 个人物:"我"和丈夫、和善的女士,都是故事的关键人物,故事的情节就围绕着这三个人物展开。

文本中的关键词有:climbing, headed for, our rental car, lost, snow 和 gratitude 等。这些词汇在续写情节的发展和形成过程中,起着非常重要的作用。

(二)提示句分析

根据第一段提示句"My husband suddenly spotted a small building on a hill in the distance"我们可以推断出,第一段的主要内容应该围绕 spot a small building 的激动心情和怎样克服身体上的种种不适走向小建筑。

根据第二段提示句"Just then, a friendly woman appeared, saying, 'Hello.'"我们可以推断出,a friendly woman 怎样帮助这对夫妇回到停车场,以及他们的感激之情,突出女士的和蔼可亲和乐于助人的品质。

五、写作思路构建

我们看到了远处的一栋小建筑,心情十分高兴,刚才的劳累一扫而光,我们朝山顶的建筑走去,来到山顶,不见任何人,心情又突然紧张起来,这时候一位和善的女士出现了,并热情地跟我们打招呼,我们说明了原因,她热情地帮我们明确了下山的方向,在高高的山顶,瞭望远处,我们看见了我们的车辆,非常感激这位女士,我们一路朝山脚下走去。

(一)习作欣赏

My husband suddenly spotted a small building on a hill in the distance. In no time did we find ourselves heading for it. We were filled with hope and excitement to find such a building in the remote area. We climbed up the hill at a swimming pace as if all the pains were gone. As we approached, a sign came into sight, which read: Administration Office. However, it was not open for business. The empty hall made us nervous all at once. We stood there hopelessly, wondering what to do next.

Just then, a friendly woman appeared, saying, "Hello." I could barely hold back my enthusiasm and blurted out, "We're lost!" She comforted us and opened a room for us to take a break. Seeing we were cold and hungry, she treated us with hot chocolate. After studying the map, we figured out that our car was parked over three kilometers away. She offered us a ride back to our car and we accepted gladly. I felt relieved to see our rental car again. I felt so blessed to have such an unforgettable experience.

（二）习作评价

续写部分和原文及提示句的融洽度高，"In no time did we find ourselves heading for it. We were filled with hope and excitement to find such a building in the remote area"的描写表达了动作的迅速和刻不容缓。紧接着就兴奋无比，然后空旷的环境使得心情起伏。和善女士的出现奠定了整个故事的美好结局。

第八节　好奇困惑

好奇、困惑的心理特征是故事中常见的。这种心理活动常常和身体语言描写结合，如果再恰当地增加直接引语，就会生动形象地刻画出好奇困惑的画面。

一、构建语料库

（一）词汇短语

1. 单词

confuse	v. 使困惑;使糊涂;混淆	curious	adj. 好奇的;奇怪的
confused	adj. 困惑的;糊涂的	puzzle	v. 使迷惑 n. 难题;谜
confusing	adj. 令人困惑的	wonder	n. 惊异;惊叹;奇迹 v. (对……)感到惊讶/好奇;想知道
curiosity	n. 好奇心		

2. 词组

satisfy/arouse sb's curiosity	满足/激起某人的好奇心
at a loss	迷茫
(be) curious about	对……很好奇
(be) curious to know	(出于好奇)想知道

go blank	头脑空白
it is curious+that 从句	……很奇怪
(It is) no wonder (that)…	不足为奇
I wonder if/whether…	(我)不知是否……
out of curiosity	出于好奇
wonder at/about	对……感到惊讶

(二)话题情景

①People gathered round, curious to know what is happening.

人们聚拢过来,很想知道发生了什么事情。

②A thousand confused thoughts come to one's mind. 千头万绪涌上心头。

③They asked me so many questions that I got confused.

他们问了我许许多多的问题,把我弄糊涂了。

④I am puzzled why you didn't try for a university scholarship.

我不理解你为什么不申请奖学金。

⑤When I stood up to speak, my mind went blank.

当我站起来讲话时,我的脑子一片空白。

(三)情景语段

When we were seated, our teacher introduced a new student from England. The moment I heard his words, a lot of questions rose from my heart: why did he come here from Britain? What was he like? Drawn by a strong sense of curiosity, everyone shifted their attention from textbook to the boy, waiting for answers. At that time, the boy made a brief but definite self-introduction, which brought out his well-going character and satisfied our curiosity.

二、语篇分析

阅读下面短文,根据内容和所给段落开头语续写两段,使之构成一个完整的短文。

It was a rough week. The price of oil skyrocketed as the temperature dropped sharply in Maine. We were looking at a high of eight degrees that week, and I had missed three days of work so my paycheck was going to be lower than normal. I was stressed, to say the least. I shopped strategically, looking for every possible way to cut pennies so I could buy groceries and keep the house warm.

My eight-year-old son didn't understand when I told him we were struggling that week. He wanted a special kind of yoghurt(酸奶), but I didn't have the extra three dollars to buy it for him. It was the kind of yoghurt with a cartoon kid riding a skateboard on the front of the box, and a mere two spoonfuls in each cup. It was the kind of product that wastes a parent's money and makes me hate advertising.

I felt guilty as a parent when those big eyes looked at me with confusion, as if to say, "It's just yoghurt. What's the big deal?" So I found a way. I put something back as single mothers often do. He got his yoghurt.

On the way back from the grocery store, I noticed a homeless man holding a sign by the side of the road. My heart hurt, and I tried not to look at him. I watched people stay away from him on the street and walk by without even meeting his eyes. I looked at him closely then — bare hands grasping a piece of cardboard, snot(鼻涕) frozen to his face, a worn out jacket. And there I was struggling because I had to buy oil and groceries. But I decided to help. I pulled over to the man and handed him a five-dollar bill.

注意:

1. 续写词数应为 150 左右

2. 请按如下格式在答题卡的相应位置作答

Seeing this, my son became confused and surprised.

On that day, my son performed an act that most adults wouldn't have done.

三、文本故事架构

本文属于"人与自我"——"做人与做事"主题语境。"我"和儿子去超市购物,八岁的儿子想买一种特别的酸奶,因为经济拮据,这让"我"很为难。回家的路上,"我"注意到一个无家可归者守在路边,"我"打算帮助他,"我"拿出了五块钱递给他。考生在阅读这类文本时,应把握故事发展的三条线,即时空线、故事情节线和情感发展线。

(一)时空线

故事发生在超市。

In the grocery store…→On the way back from the grocery store 等。

(二)故事情节线

温度下降,燃油价格飙升,我三天没有工作了,我的压力很大,买东西仔细盘算着花最少的钱,买最多的东西。八岁的儿子不明白这些,去超市他想买一种特别的酸奶,我没有多余的三块钱给他买酸奶,超市里的父母用困惑的眼神看着我的时候,他们的眼光好像是在说,"不就是一杯酸奶吗?"我感到非常内疚。我找到了解决问题的办法,把选好的东西放到货架上,这样就有了钱给他买了酸奶。回家的路上,我注意到一个无家可归者守在路边,他穿着破烂,人们纷纷躲避不及,而我打算帮助他,我拿出了五块钱递给他。

（三）情感发展线

进超市购物,儿子买酸奶(内疚为难)→回家路上,遇见穿着破烂无家可归者,众人漠视(无情)→我打算帮助他(善良)。

四、关键信息梳理

（一）人物

语篇出现了 3 个人物:"我"、八岁的儿子和无家可归者,都是关键人物。

文本中的关键词有 Paycheck, stressed, yoghurt, my eight-year-old son, struggling, money, a homeless man, groceries 和 help 等。这些词汇在续写情节的形成和发展过程中,起着非常重要的作用。

（二）提示句分析

根据第一段提示句"Seeing this, my son became confused and surprised"我们可以推断出,这一段续写儿子的困惑和惊讶,儿子一定会问"我"为什么这么做。在这一过程中,"我"跟儿子解释,让他明白"我"做事的道理,也是在教育孩子。

根据第二段提示句"On that day, my son performed an act that most adults wouldn't have done"我们可以推断出,这主要是写儿子听了"我"的解释以后,他做了意想不到的事情,又因为本文的重点线索是酸奶,因此我们可以推断出儿子把酸奶送给了无家可归者。

五、写作思路构建

看见我把五块钱递给陌生的无家可归者,儿子非常困惑,非常惊讶。"妈妈,为什么你没有钱给我买酸奶? 而把五块钱交给陌生人呢?"我认真地跟儿子解释:如果不帮助他,他会饿死的。而不喝酸奶,人照样可以成长。那一天,儿子做了大部分成年人也做不到的一件事情。他认真地看了看手中的酸奶,然后把酸奶送给了路边的无家可归者,并祝福无家可归者每天快乐。

（一）习作欣赏

<u>Seeing this, my son became confused and surprised.</u> "Mum, why you are so generous to a stranger while so mean to me when I asked for the yoghurt?" I explained that if I were blind to his poor situation, the man could be freezing. He didn't have a home or something to eat after all. I felt like I could spare five dollars even if I was financially stressed. Finally my son nodded and fixed his eyes on the yoghurt.

<u>On that day, my son performed an act that most adults wouldn't have done.</u> He took his yoghurt out of the bag in the back seat and handed it to the gentleman outside his window. Even if it was just a matter of a few spoonfuls of yoghurt, it was all he had, and he gave it to someone who needed it more than he wanted it. He showed me that I am doing well as a mother. There are always blessings to count if we open our eyes, and that we always have the opportunity to be a blessing for someone else.

（二）习作评价

续写部分情节设计合理,语言的融洽度高。本文中的关键线索酸奶贯穿全文,男孩把心爱的酸奶送给无家可归者,深情地传递了爱的含义。第一段开头,男孩面对困惑和好奇的质问,符合孩子的天真的特点。总的来说,文章语言丰富,句型多样,体现出了作者语言运用的灵活性与扎实的英语语言能力。

第九节　安慰宽慰

安慰、宽慰指的是安顿抚慰,用欢娱、希望、保证以及同理心减轻、安抚或鼓励。可以侧重手的动作,也可以侧重眼神的信息传递;也可以在言语上进行安抚或者鼓励,等等。

一、构建语料库

(一)词汇短语

1. 单词

comfort	n. 慰藉;令人安慰的人或物 v. 安慰	relieved	adj. 感到宽慰的
considerate	adj. 体贴的;考虑周到的	sensible	adj. 明智的;合理的;可觉察到的
relieve	v. 使减轻;使解除(痛苦、忧愁等)	sensitive	adj. 善解人意的;(感情)敏感的
relief	n. (痛苦等的)减轻;宽慰	thoughtfully	adv. 沉思地;亲切地;体贴地

2. 词组

at ease	舒适;自在
be considerate to/towards sb.	对某人很体贴
be content with	满足……
be sensitive to sb.	体谅某人
be sensitive to sth.	对某事敏感
bend down	弯下腰来
breathe/let out a deep sigh	发出深深的叹息
cast comforting glance at sb.	投去安慰的目光
hold/hug sb. in one's arms	搂在怀中
look sb. gently in the eye	温柔地看着
nod at sb.	微笑向某人点头
pat sb. on the shoulder	轻轻拍着肩膀
sigh with relief	如释重负地叹气
smiling down at	微笑地看着
throw one's arms around sb. tightly without hesitation	毫不犹豫地抱住

(二)话题情景

①She didn't say a word, but smiled a watery smile and held my hand tightly.

她一句话也没说,只是微微一笑,紧紧握住我的手。

②She stroked her fingers through my hair, and said, "Things are going to be fine."

她用手指抚摸着我的头发,说:"一切都会好的。"

③The woman was staring at the girl, wiping out tears from her cheeks.

那个女人正盯着那个女孩,擦掉脸颊上的眼泪。

④He reached out his hand, with his finger forming a heart, saying "I will always be there with you."

他伸出手,手指形成一颗"心",说:"我永远在你身边。"

⑤They are sitting outside in the cool night on a wooden porch, comforting and encouraging each other quietly.

他们坐在外面凉爽的夜晚,在木廊上,静静地安慰和鼓励对方。

⑥Seeing her condition (pain), I immediately felt a huge of sympathy for her. It was coming deep from with in my heart.

看到她的处境,我立刻从我的内心深处对她产生了巨大的同情。

⑦Let bygones be bygones. 过去的就让它过去吧。

⑧Life is not all roses. 人生并不是康庄大道。

⑨All things come to those who wait. 苍天不负有心人。

(三)情景语段

I failed the exam. When I got home, mom was preparing dinner. I throw myself in the chair, eyes blank and in tears. Seeing that, mom paced towards me and expressed her care. I pulled out all the whole story, crying in her arms. Gently and softly, mom said: "It doesn't matter whether it is a failure or success. It is your dedicated attempt that values most. The dinner is your reward!" Through mom's comforting words and the delicious dinner, I felt relieved and gained meaningful lessons.

二、语篇分析

阅读下面短文,根据内容和所给段落开头语续写两段,使之构成一个完整的短文。

Mother's gift

I grew up in a small town where the primary school was a ten-minute walk from my house. When the noon bell rang, I would race breathlessly home. My mother would be standing at the top of the stairs, smiling down at me.

One lunch time when I was in the third grade will stay with me always. I had been picked to be the princess in the school play, and for weeks my mother had rehearsed my lines so hard with me. But no matter how easily I acted at home, as soon as I stepped on stage, every word disappeared from my head. Finally, my teacher took me aside. She explained that she had written a narrator's part to the play, and asked me to change roles. Her word, kindly expressed, still hurt, especially when I saw my part go to another girl.

I didn't tell my mother what had happened when I went home for lunch that day. But she sensed my pain. Instead of suggesting we practice my lines, she asked if I wanted to walk in the yard.

It was a lovelyspring day and the rose vine was turning green. Under the huge trees, we could see yellow dandelions (蒲公英) in the grass in bunch as if a painter had touched our landscape with some gold. I watched my mother casually bend down by one dandelion. "I think I'm going to dig up all these weeds," she said, pulling it up by its roots. "From now on, we'll have only roses in this garden."

"But I like dandelions," I protested. "All flowers are beautiful—even dandelions."

My mother looked at me seriously. "Yes, every flower gives pleasure in its own way, doesn't it?" She asked thoughtfully. I nodded, pleased that I had won her over. "And that is true of people too," she added. "Not everyone can be a princess, but there is no shame in that." Relieved that she had guessed my pain, I started to cry as I told her what had happened. She listened and smiled reassuringly (安慰地).

注意：

1. 续写词数应为 150 左右

2. 请按如下格式在答题卡的相应位置作答

> "But you will be a beautiful narrator," Mother said.
>
> After the play, I took home the flower.

三、文本故事架构

本文属于"人与自我"——"认识自我、丰富自我、完善自我"主题语境。主要写"我"在儿时失意的时候，经过母亲的引导，"我"终于醒悟成长的故事。考生在阅读这类文本时，应把握故事发展的三条线，即时空线、故事情节线和情感发展线。

（一）时空线

故事发生在学校,在家中。

One lunchtime when I was in the third grade … → when I went home for lunch that day 等。

（二）故事情节线

我一开始被老师选为话剧表演的主角。但是由于自己台词现场表现能力欠缺,最终被换成旁白的角色。在受了打击之后,母亲感受到了我内心中的失落。她带我来到花园里,通过比较艳丽夺目的玫瑰和平凡温馨的蒲公英,让我明白一个道理——每个人都有自己的美丽,母亲的言语对我的人生产生重要影响。

（三）情感发展线

每天放学飞奔回家,投入母亲的怀抱(依赖母亲)→学校选角色,母亲陪我一起训练(信任母亲)→临场能力欠佳,角色被替换(失落)→妈妈领我进公园用蒲公英启迪(鼓励)→我彻底明白了道理(感激)。

四、关键信息梳理

（一）人物

语篇中主要人物就是"我"、母亲和老师,最主要人物是"我"和母亲。

文本中关键词有:I, mother, kindly, lovely, dandelions, beautiful, flower, smile, mother 是本文的主人公, dandelion 和 flower 其实是关键信息词, kindly, smile 体现妈妈的性格特征。

（二）提示句分析

从续写篇章的第一句"'But you will be a beautiful narrator,'she said"来看,作者的母亲说话内容以及意义是本段的核心。前文那句话的 beautiful 的用词,可以推测母亲的鼓励与支持,关爱。

从第二句"After the play, I took home the flower"可以看出,关键词是"flower",作者拿着这朵花回家,会对这朵花有特殊的珍藏以及对母亲的感激。

五、写作思路构建

标题 Mother's gift 既指母亲给予作者的礼物本身——蒲公英,又指通过这件事给予作者的鼓励与爱。母亲对作者的人生产生了深远的影响。

母亲鼓励作者的时候,用 beautiful 这个词表达了妈妈的情感。妈妈鼓励孩子的同时会加以轻柔温和的肢体动作,才能充分体现出对作者的关心与爱。

从第二段中的关键词"flower"出发,可以反推第一段中母亲肯定赠予作者一朵花,结合前文的分析,这朵花就是一朵蒲公英。作者对母亲这种"以花代人"的做法表示感激。正是因为此次"蒲公英"的特殊意义,作者可能会珍藏蒲公英花,蒲公英花是母亲的化身,是对于未来整个人生的一种感悟。

（一）习作欣赏

"But you will be a beautiful narrator," Mother said. She encouraged and comforted me as always as she did. My beloved mom, wearing a shining smile on her face, added. "The narrator's part is important, too." Thanks to her encouragement, which calmed me down gradually, and I began to accept the narrator part was of vital significance. Time went so fast that it reached to the performance day. At first I was still nervous, but it was at that very moment that I found a dandelion in my pocket. I knew my mom passed the flower to me, which meant to be in company with me.

After the play, I took home the flower. Mom carefully looked at the dandelion, gently pressed it into the dictionary and smiled happily as she did. "We were perhaps the only people who would press such a sorry-looking weed." Though decades have passed, I constantly recall our precious lunchtime being together, clinging to each other, bathed in the soft mid daylight. For this, I am forever grateful, because smiles on mother's face and her kind act foster a man like me now! And all those inspiring words like "Cease to struggle and you cease to live" have been echoing in my mind as fresh as a daisy.

（二）习作评价

续写部分描写温情,感人。本文中的关键线索蒲公英一直贯穿于文章中,体现了蒲公英的价值,在传递这朵花的同时,也深深地传递着母女之情。第一段对于人物的面部表情描写细致入微,在形容词的选用上,细致到位,例如 beloved, shining;在副词的选择上,也比较丰富地体现了动词的性质与意义,例如 gradually, carefully, happily, constantly,等等。在安慰女儿的话语中,文章用了"Cease to struggle and you cease to live",体现出母亲对女儿的鼓励与期望。总的来说,文章语言丰富,句型多样,体现出了作者语言运用的灵活性与扎实的英语语言能力。

第十节　孤独郁闷

孤独、郁闷的心情是在外界或者内在心理活动的前提下的负面心理反应,这种心理通常伴随着某些肢体语言。

一、构建语料库

(一)词汇短语

1. 单词

alone	adj.独自一人的,独自的	frown	n.皱眉;不悦 v.不同意;皱眉头
bored	adj.厌烦的;烦闷的	lone	adj.孤单的;唯一的;单独的
boring	adj.无聊的;令人厌烦	lonely	adj.孤独的;寂寞的
darken	v.变暗;使阴郁;使变暗	loneliness	n.孤独;寂寞
deserted	adj.废弃的;荒芜的;被遗弃的	pitiful	adj.慈悲的;可怜的;凄惨的
despair	n.绝望	upset	adj.心烦的;苦恼的;不安的 v.使心烦
depress	vt.使沮丧;使萧条;压抑	desperate	adj.绝望的;不顾一切的

2. 词组

(be) bored with	对……感到厌倦
drag one's feet	拖着双脚

(二)话题情景

①I couldn't help being self-pitying. 我忍不住自怜起来。

②A wave of loneliness washed over her. 她感到了一阵阵寂寞。

③I thought to myself, upset and gloomy.
我心里想着,心烦意乱,闷闷不乐。

④He stood right in front of me with his head down.
他低着头,站在我面前。

⑤Cold with no hope for warmth, she felt like drowning in a crowd of people.
冷得连温暖的希望都没有,她觉得自己就像浸没在人群之中。

⑥Not content with life, I have a good reason to frown, for the world was intended to drag me down.

不满足于生活,我有充足的理由沮丧,因为这个世界本来是想让我沮丧的。

⑦I realized I was becoming increasingly depressed.

我觉得自己越来越抑郁。

(三)情景语段

I was unfamiliar with my new classmates and this new school. Feeling like an isolated island, I was consumed by a flood of loneliness all day. With no friends to pour out my happiness or trouble, I found myself increasingly inactive, silent and depressed day by day. That was not what I wanted to be! Thus, picking up my courage, I made up my mind to adapt to the new school and get to know my new classmates as quickly as possible.

二、语篇分析

阅读下面短文,根据内容和所给段落开头语续写两段,使之构成一个完整的短文。

In Your Eyes

The park bench was deserted as is at down to read beneath the long branches of an old willow tree. I was deserted. Endless quarrels with my family had left me nowhere to go but this lonely corner of the park. As I sat on the bench, things happened recently began to flash through. Days seemed months to me recently. No cozy home to stay. No happy memories with family. No considerate family members to talk to. Even the book I was reading was no fun. Not content with life, I had a good reason to frown, for the world was intended to drag me down.

And if that weren't enough to ruin my day, a young boy out of breath approached me, all tired from play. He stood right in front of me with his head tilted down and said with great excitement, "Look what I found!" In his hand was a flower. What a pitiful sight, its petals(花瓣) were all worn—not enough rain, or too little light. He must have picked the flower from somewhere shady and sunless, just like where I was staying these days. I couldn't help being self-pitying. Wanting him to take his dead flower away and go off to play, I faked a small smile and then looked away. "Why couldn't everyone just leave me be!" I thought to myself, upset and gloomy.

But instead of leaving, he sat next to my side and placed the flower to his nose and declared loudly with certainty, "It sure smells pretty and it must be beautiful, too. That's why I picked it; here, it's for you." The weed before me was dying or dead, not vibrant of colors, orange, yellow or red. But I knew I must take it, or he might never leave. So I reached for the flower, and replied, "Just what I need." Again, instead of placing the flower in my hand, he held it mid-air without reason or plan.

Curiosity drove me to look into his eyes. Blue as the sea, there is no color of light in his beautiful eyes.

注意：

1. 续写词数应为 150 左右

2. 请按如下格式在答题卡的相应位置作答

> It was then that I noticed for the very first time that the boy was blind. For all of those times I myself had been blind towards the world around me.

三、文本故事架构

本文属于"人与自我"——"认识自我、丰富自我、完善自我"主题语境。主要记叙了作者"我"在公园长椅上与一个盲人小男孩的交流让"我"改变了人生态度的经历。考生在阅读这类文本时，应把握故事发展的三条线，即时空线、故事情节线和情感发展线。

（一）时空线

故事发生的地点是在公园。我坐到椅子上与男孩交谈后，男孩离开。

（二）故事情节线

因为家庭争吵，我来到公园，坐在长椅上看书，心情郁闷。小男孩来到我面前，兴奋地和我分享他找到的这朵残败凋零的花。出于礼貌，我回应了他，希望他快点离开。但是他却坐到我身边，赞美这朵花的美丽，并且想要把这朵花送给我。这时我才发现这个小男孩是一个盲人。我深受震撼，也深受感动。小男孩虽然双目失明，却能够看到生活的美好，并且将这份美好传递给他人。我意识到自己要学会去看生活中美好积极的一面。

（三）情感发展线

文本重点呈现的是"我"的情绪和人生态度的改变。

我到公园，坐在长椅上看书（心情郁闷，自怨自怜）→一个小男孩前来兴奋地和我分享残败凋零的花,我希望他快点离开(无奈)→他却坐到我身边,再次赞美这朵花的美丽,并且想要把这朵花送给我(心烦)→发现这个小男孩是一个盲人(震撼)。

四、关键信息梳理

(一)人物

语篇中的主要的人物是"我"和小男孩。

文本中的关键词有:willow tree,boy,self-pitying,smile,flower,eyes 等。这些词汇在续写故事情节的形成和发展过程中,起着非常重要的作用。抓住了这些关键词就抓住了续写的思路。

(二)提示句分析

从第一段首句"It was then that I noticed for the very first time that the boy could not see:he was blind"的提示,我们可以推断出,"我"意识到小男孩是一个盲人,深感惊讶与感动。因此,续写的第一段应该重点将"我"惊讶与感动的情绪描写出来。

根据第二段首句"For all of those times I myself had been blind towards the world around me"的提示,我们可以推断出,小男孩善意的举动使"我"意识到自己负面情绪的不足。因此,本段应该着重描写看到小男孩的举动之后,"我"意识到的具体内容,并为此做出怎么样的行动,而"我"抑郁、烦闷的心情是如何改变的。

五、写作思路构建

本文 In Your Eyes 的含义指的是小男孩眼中的世界。小男孩双目失明,但他看到了美丽的世界,并向周围的人传递了这份美;我从小男孩的身上学习到应该以乐观积极的态度去面对生活中的困难。

我被小男孩虽然失明却还能感知美,传播美的善意所惊讶与感动。我因为内心的震撼而感动落泪,稳定情绪后向小男孩表达感激之情,并思考小男孩到底是如何发现我的困境,之后才发现其实这个小男孩向他能接触的每个人都传递了这份美丽的善意。闻着手里玫瑰的芬芳,我意识到,只要用心去感知,就能积极发现生活中的美好。

(一)习作欣赏

It was then that I noticed for the very first time that the boy was blind. I heard my voice trembling. Tears shone like the sun as I thanked him for picking the very best flower. "You're welcome,"he smiled,and then ran off to play,not realizing the

impact he'd had on my day. I sat there and wondered how he managed to see a self
-pitying woman beneath an old willow tree. How did he know of my trouble?
Perhaps he'd been blessed with true sight from his heart by God.

For all of those times I myself had been blind towards the world around me.
Through the eyes of a blind boy, at last I could see the problem was not with the
world; the problem was me. I decided and promised to see beauty, and appreciate
every second of my life. Then I held that dead flower up to my nose and breathed
in the fragrance of a beautiful rose, smiling like that young boy. "That is the best
flower, and I'm grateful."

（二）习作评价

两段续写的重心在人物情绪的变化上，勾勒出"我"阴郁孤单的心境，同
时也与下文用 appreciate，smile 等词勾勒出的感恩欣喜的心情形成对比。情
绪的对比描写侧面展现出人物价值观的转变，同时也完成了主题的升华。

第十一节　惊讶尴尬

惊讶、尴尬的心理首先是表现在脸上的，然后可能延伸到肢体上。表现
惊讶、尴尬的感情，主要通过动作描写来体现。

一、构建语料库

（一）词汇短语

1.单词

amaze	v.使大为吃惊;使感到惊愕	astonish	v.使人为惊讶;使惊骇
amazed	adj.吃惊的;惊奇的	shock	n.震惊;令人震惊的事 v.使震惊
amazing	adv.令人惊喜地	surprise	n.惊奇;使人吃惊的事 v.使惊奇

2.词组

（be）amazed to find	了解到……感到吃惊
be numb with shock	惊呆了
beyond words	难以言喻的
beyond one's expectations	出乎某人意料地

go mad with joy	欣喜若狂
in amazement/astonishment/surprise/shock	吃惊地
It surprises/shocks/amazes sb. that…	使人惊奇的是……
take…by surprise	使……吃惊;空袭
to one's amazement / astonishment	让某人惊讶的
with her mouth wide open	张大嘴巴

（二）话题情景

①She stood besides her chair, surprised and embarrassed.

她站在椅子旁边,又惊讶又尴尬。

②She froze, her mouth hanging open. 她呆住了,嘴巴张开着。

③She cupped her face with her hands, scratched her head, breathed and breathed until she felt calm.

她用手托着脸,挠挠头,不停地呼吸,直到感到平静下来。

④She lowered a bit of her body, hesitated for a moment, wondering how to hide her inner embarrassment.

她微微低下身子,犹豫了一会儿,在想如何去掩饰内心的尴尬。

⑤She opened her mouth with her eyes widening and face turning red.

她张大着嘴巴,同时瞪着眼睛,脸顿时变红。

⑥Suddenly, she leaped up, embarrassment in her red face.

突然,她跳了起来,涨红的脸上流露出窘迫。

⑦All the air seemed to disappear and she felt as if the whole world was watching her.

所有的空气似乎都消失了,她觉得整个世界好像都在注视着她。

（三）情景语段

When I knew the truth, I stood there like a stone, surprised and embarrassed. I asked myself silently in my heart, "Why could it be this?" Then I felt the blood rush to my face like it was burning. My lips were tight and my mind was blank, a little at a loss.

二、语篇分析

阅读下面短文,根据内容和所给段落开头语续写两段,使之构成一个完整的短文。

A Boy and His Father Become Partners

I like all kinds of chocolate. Best of all, though, I like bitter baking chocolate. Mother had bought a bar of it, and somehow I couldn't stop thinking about it.

I was helping father on the winnower(扬谷器). It was right then I got the idea. I could cut cut off the end of that bar of chocolate. Mother would be sure miss it, but before she had any idea who had done it, I could confess I'd taken it. Probably I would not even get a spanking(打屁股).

I waited until mother was out feeding the chickens. Then I told father I thought I'd go in for a drink of water. I got the bar down but I heard mother coming just when I had the knife ready to cut. So I slipped the chocolate into the front of my shirt and left quickly. Before I went back to help father, I went to the barn and hid the chocolate there.

I told myself that I hadn't really stolen the whole bar of chocolate, because I meant to take only a little piece. If I put back the whole bar, I wouldn't have done anything wrong at all.

I nearly decided to put it all back. But just thinking so much about chocolate made my tongue almost taste the smooth bitterness of it. I got thinking that if I slice about half an inch off the end with a sharp knife? Mother might never notice it.

I was nearly out to where the cows were when I remembered what father had said once—some of the family money was mine because I had helped to earn it. Why wouldn't it be all right to figure the bar of chocolate had been bought with my own money? That seemed to fix everything.

That night I couldn't sleep. At last I got up, slipped out into the yard, and took the ax from the chopping block. Then I secretly went into the barn and got the chocolate. I took it outside and laid it on the lower rail of the corral fence. The moon gave enough light for me to see what I was doing.

注意：

1. 续写词数应为 150 左右

2. 请按如下格式在答题卡的相应位置作答

> Just as I was starting to cut, father said: "Son!"
>
> "Giving me a punishment," my father said, "You shouldn't have done it that way."

三、文本故事架构

本文属于"人与自我"——"做人与做事"主题语境。"我"喜欢吃巧克力,但最喜欢的是有苦味的巧克力,妈妈买了这样的巧克力,"我"就忍不住想吃。偷了巧克力进了谷仓,正要用刀切下一点点却被爸爸发现了。考生在阅读这类文本时,应把握故事发展的三条线,即时空线、故事情节线和情感发展线。

(一)时空线

故事发生在家中。

I was helping father on the winnower when I got the idea→slipped the chocolate into the front of my shirt and left quickly→to the barn and hid the chocolate there→That night I got up,slipped out into the yard and took the ax→Then I secretly went into the barn to cut the chocolate。

(二)故事情节线

我喜欢吃巧克力,但最喜欢的是苦味的巧克力,妈妈买了这样的巧克力,我就忍不住想吃。那时,我在农场帮助爸爸妈妈干活,我有这样的想法,就是从巧克力上切一块,或许不会被发现。终于等到机会来了,有个夜晚我没有睡觉,拿了一把刀子,带着巧克力,溜到院子里,偷偷进了谷仓,我告诉自己,我不是真的想偷巧克力,我只是想切一点。我靠着篱笆,月光正好让我看清楚要切的巧克力。

(三)情感发展线

妈妈买了有苦味的巧克力,我就忍不住想吃(酷爱)→晚上偷偷拿着巧克力进谷仓切一点(迫切)。

四、关键信息梳理

(一)人物

语篇出现了 3 个人物,但关键人物是爸爸和"我"。

在文本中的关键词有:chocolate,cut off,slipped,steal,barn,get a spanking 等。这些词汇在续写情节的发展和形成过程中,起着非常重要的作用。

(二)提示句分析

根据第一段提示句"Just as I was starting to cut,father said:'Son!'我们可以推断出,主要写"我"偷切巧克力被父亲发现,接受惩罚。本段落也重点描述自己的心理活动。

根据第二段提示句"'Giving me a punishment,' my father said,'You shouldn't have done it that way.'"我们可以推断出，写爸爸对"我"的教育，使"我"认清"我"的错误。

五、写作思路构建

(一)思路一

我正想切巧克力，这时候爸爸大声说"儿子，住手!"我在篱笆边怔住了。手里拿着巧克力，人赃俱获，我知道，这次爸爸不会饶过我的。爸爸痛恨地打了我屁股，我实在是痛苦难忍。

爸爸给了我应有的惩罚。他接着说你不应该用这种方式得到巧克力，他让我明白，我应该接受惩罚，爸爸告诉我人生的道理。爸爸说，我拿巧克力不是问题，但是不应该背着他偷。疼痛过后，我也明白了爸爸的用意。

(二)思路二

我正想切巧克力，这时候爸爸大声说"儿子，住手!"我在篱笆边怔住了，非常惊讶，也非常尴尬。一阵慌乱之后，我把巧克力藏在了胸前，然后转过身来，只见到爸爸那生气的表情。我害怕爸爸痛打我一顿，我没有真的想偷整块的巧克力，我只想切下一点点。

爸爸给了我应有的惩罚。然后他接着说你不应该用这种方式得到巧克力，他让我明白，我应该接受惩罚，爸爸告诉我人生的道理。爸爸说，我拿巧克力不是问题，但是不应该背着他偷。疼痛过后，我也明白了爸爸的用意。

(三)习作欣赏

Just as I was starting to cut, father said:"Son!" I froze besides the fence, surprised and embarrassed. I couldn't think of a thing to say. In a panic, I grabbed up the bar of chocolate and immediately hid it next to my chest before I turned around. I saw Father had an angry expression on his face. I was afraid he would give me a good spanking. Then next he let me stand against the wall, standing in the darkness for a long time for a punishment! Thank God he didn't give me spanking.

"Giving me a punishment," my father said, "You shouldn't have done it that way." Then he stood me on my feet and asked if I thought I had deserved the punishment. I whispered yes. He said it wasn't so much that I'd taken the chocolate, but that I'd tried to hide it from him. I could have had it if I had asked for it. But never did something secretly rather than openly. This was a lesson I should keep in mind forever.

（四）习作评价

两段续写的重心放在心理描写上,勾勒出人物的惊讶、尴尬、慌乱,痛苦和明白事理的过程。Froze,grabbed,hid,turned around 等词形象、贴切。最后的句子展现出人物价值观的转变,同时也完成了主题的升华。

第十二节　紧张焦虑

紧张、焦虑的心理活动是读后续写故事经常遇到的情景。要善于积累相关的词汇和句式。

一、构建语料库

（一）词汇短语

1. 单词

anxiety	n. 焦虑;烦恼	tense/tens	adj. (神经)紧张的;担心的
anxious	adj. 焦虑的;渴望的	tension	n. 紧张;烦躁;(局势、关系)紧张
nerve	n. 神经紧张;焦躁	unease	adj. 不自在的 心神不安的
nervous	adj. 紧张的;不安的	worry	n. 烦恼(人事情);焦虑 v. 使焦虑;使担忧 ;困扰
restless	adj. 焦躁的、不安的	worried	adj. 焦虑的,担心的

2. 词组

a worried look	焦虑的神情
be anxious for sb. /about sth.	为某人/某事忧虑
(be) anxious to do sth.	渴望做某事
be worried about	担心……
get ants in the pants	坐立不安
heart beat wildly	心跳很快
pace up and down	踱来踱去
palms got sweaty	手心出汗
put pressure on sb.	给某人施加压力

relieve stress	缓解压力
tighten one's face	绷紧了脸
under pressure	在压力下

(二)话题情景

①His heartbeat wildly and his legs trembled.

他的心跳剧烈跳动,腿打着战。

②His face turned pale and stood there tongue-tied.

他的脸色苍白,站在那儿说不出话来。

③He felt so nervous that he couldn't move an inch.

他很紧张,一步也挪不动。

④Scared and nervous, she was frozen to the spot.

她怔在了现场,即害怕又紧张。

⑤A flood of tension welled up in him. /Tension flooded over him.

他心里涌起一股紧张情绪。

⑥The fear was like an electric shock, making his hair stand on end.

他害怕的像遭到了电击一样,毛发直竖。

⑦His heart beat so violently that he felt like sitting on pins and needles.

他的心跳剧烈跳动,如坐针毡。

⑧He tightened his face as if protecting himself against another disappointment.

他绷着脸,好像是防备另外一次失望。

⑨"How tiresome it must be to stay at home on a holiday!" said Rose, shaking her head.

"待在家里度假一定很烦人!"Rose 摇摇头说。

(三)情景语段

Angela dragged her legs and moved out of the test center, her head dropped. An air of frustration and depression could be sensed ten yards away. Soon, her eyes began to water. She would fail the math exam, definitely! Disappointment came in waves and at length, tears streamed down her face. The only thing she was eager to do was to rush back home and drop herself onto the shabby little couch and weep!

二、语篇分析

阅读下面短文,根据内容和所给段落开头语续写两段,使之构成一个完整的短文。

The Rude Boy

James Selton was one of the rudest boys in the village where he lived. If a person in the street was well dressed, he would cry out, "Dandy(花花公子)!" If a person's clothes were dirty or torn, he would throw stones at him, and annoy him in every way.

One afternoon, just as the school was dismissed, a stranger passed through the village. His dress was plain and somewhat old, but neat and clean. He carried a cane in his hand, on the end of which was a bundle, and he wore abroad-brimmed hat.

No sooner had James seen the stranger than he winked to his playmates, and said, "Now for some fun!" He then silently went toward the stranger from behind, and, knocking off his hat, ran away.

The man turned and saw him, but James was far away before he could speak. The stranger put on his hat, and went on his way. Again did James approach; but this time, the man caught him by the arm, and held him tightly. However, he contented himself with looking James a moment in the face, and then pushed him from him. No sooner had the naughty boy found himself free again than he began to threw at the stranger with dirt and stones.

But James was much frightened when the man was struck on the head by a brick. All the boys now ran away, and James skulked (躲躲闪闪) across the fields to his home.

As he drew near the house, his sister Caroline came out to meet him, holding up a beautiful gold chain and some new books for him to see. She told James that their uncle, who had been away several years, had come home, and was now in the house; that he had brought beautiful presents for the whole family; that he had left his carriage at the tavern(客栈), a mile or two off, and walked on foot, so as to surprise his brother, their father.

注意:

1. 续写词数应为 150 左右
2. 请按如下格式在答题卡的相应位置作答

> She said someill boys threw stones at him on the road.
> His uncle went up to him and felt surprised.

三、文本故事架构

本文属于"人与自我"——"认识自我、丰富自我、完善自我"主题语境。记叙了一位粗鲁无礼的男孩 James 的恶作剧伤害了多年未曾谋面的叔叔,最后醒悟后悔,从而改变捉弄人的坏习惯的经历。考生在阅读这类文本时,应把握故事发展的三条线,即时空线、故事情节线和情感发展线。

(一)时空线

故事发生的地点从大街上和家中。

One afternoon, just as the school was dismissed…→As she drew near the house 等。

(二)故事情节线

放学后,顽劣的小男孩 James 用石头砸伤大街上的陌生人,后来到家门口妹妹告知多年未见面的叔叔来看望他们一家人,并带来了很多礼物。

(三)情感发展线

James 是欺负别人的调皮男生。砸伤陌生人后,James 感到害怕的心理。从第一段的首句提示我们可以推断出,当妹妹告诉 James,多年未见的叔叔被调皮的孩子砸伤时,James 一定已经猜测出那个他用石头砸伤的陌生人就是自己的叔叔,他会心生后悔之意。从第二段首句的提示,我们可以推断出,叔叔一番话或者父母的行为,让 James 明白应该如何来改变自己行为。情感线的发展是从开心玩闹→害怕→后悔→醒悟的过程。

四、关键信息梳理

(一)人物

语篇中的关键人物是 James、uncle 和 father。

文本中的关键词有:rudest, street, stranger, went, James, approach, struck, uncle, presents 和 father 等。

James 是本文主人公,stranger、uncle 是主人公 James 的成长经历的关键人物和文章线索,是必选词汇;本文父亲的行为推动着故事情节的发展,father 也是必选词。rudest 是主人公原来的性格特点。went, approach, struck 是主人公动作的备选用词,可以考虑嵌入情节中,起烘托氛围的作用。

（二）提示句分析

从第一段首句"She said while he was coming through the village, some wicked boys threw stones at him"的提示，我们可以推断出，上文受伤的陌生人一定是 James 的叔叔。结合妹妹的话和上文告知的 James 害怕的心理，续写的第一段应该描写 James 不敢立即去面对叔叔和父母的愧疚心理以及把相应的行为描写出来。

从第二段首句"His uncle went up to him and felt surprised"的提示，我们可以推断出，第二段应该聚焦在叔叔的惊讶和宽恕，James 的自我反思，或者父母所采取的一系列行为上。

五、写作思路构建

听到妹妹的话，James 意识到自己伤害了叔叔，不敢走进房子里面，站在门口发现妈妈正在给叔叔包扎伤口。妈妈发现他后，叫他进来，并介绍这是叔叔，告知他叔叔给他带来礼物。叔叔走向 James，发现 James 是肇事男孩，但没有明说。James 自我反省，羞愧难当，主动告知父母，父母和叔叔原谅了他。

（一）习作欣赏

She said some ill boys threw stones at him on the road. Hearing this, the guilty boy ran into the house and went upstairs quickly. Soon after, he heard his father calling him to come down. Trembling from head to foot, he obeyed. He stood there with his head down, nervous and frightened. His mother said, "James see this beautiful watch-your uncle has brought for you." What a sense of shame did James feel now! Little Caroline seized his arm and pulled him into the room, But he hung down his head.

His uncle went up to him and felt surprised. It was the boy who so badly treated him in the street! James' heart beat so violently that he felt like sitting on pins and needles. He was frightened to be treated as he treated his uncle. However, he was relieved to find his uncle would forgive him. But his father would never permit James to have any presents from his uncle. James was obliged to content himself with seeing them happy. He never forgot this lesson so long as he lived. It cured him entirely of his low and insolent rude manners.

（二）习作评价

主人公 James 的动作和心理，母亲的语言和妹妹 Caroline 的动作都非常吻合各自的身份和性格特征。hearing, trembling 做伴随状语，结合主体动词的描写,增强了叙事的画面感,并推动了故事情节的发展。trembling from head to foot 做伴随状语的运用,体现了主人公内心的紧张害怕。Be obliged to content himself with seeing them happy 把主人公的"无奈后悔"的心理表现得淋漓尽致,自然水到渠成地得出文章的结尾。

第十三节　痛苦忧伤

　　有各种各样的失败,有失意,或者无法承受的压力就有痛苦和忧伤。痛苦、忧伤的心理活动是读后续写故事经常遇到的情景,要善于积累相关的词汇和句式。

一、构建语料库

(一)词汇短语

1. 单词

affect	vt. 影响;感动	heartbroken	adj. 心碎的
bitter	adj. 痛苦的;充满仇恨的;(味道)苦的	hopeless	adj. 绝望的;没有希望的
blue	adj. 悲伤的;忧郁的	horrible	adj. 可怕的;极讨厌的
bother	v. 使烦恼;费心;麻烦;打扰	sorrow	n. 悲伤;悲痛
depress	v. 使抑郁;使沮丧	sorry	adj. 难过的;抱歉的
depressed	adj. 抑郁的;沮丧的	tremble	v & n. 颤抖;哆嗦
desperate	adj. 绝望的;孤注一掷的;极度渴望的	relief	n. (痛苦等的)减轻;宽慰
disappoint	v. 使失望	relieve	v. 使减轻;使解除(痛苦、忧愁等)
disappointed	adj. 失望的;沮丧的	unhappy	adj. 不幸福的;不愉快的
discouraged	adj. 沮丧的	upset	adj. 心烦意乱的 v. 使生气(心烦意乱)
down	adj. 沮丧的;情绪低落的	weep	v. 流泪;哭泣

2. 词组

be affected by	被……感动;受……影响
be lost in sorrow / be overcome with sorrow	沉浸在悲伤中
blue with cold	冻得发青
bother sb. about/with	……使某人烦恼
burst into tears	突然大哭
choke with sob	嗓子哽住
cry for/over sth.	为……哭泣
disappoint sb.'s expectations	辜负某人的期望
float in an ocean of sadness	沉浸在悲伤的海洋中
head drooping	低着头
have a good cry	好好哭了一场
hide one's face in her hands	把头埋在手里
in low spirits	意志消沉
lose heart	灰心
let sb. down	使失望;辜负
sob one's heart out	哭得死去活来
tears roll down her cheeks	泪流满面
to one's relief	使某人宽慰的是
weep for/over sth.	为……哭泣

(二)话题情景

①She lay on the bed, weeping in pain. 她躺在床上, 痛得呜咽不已。

②I saw an old lady crying with fist beating her chest in the street corner.
我看见一个老太太在街角处捶胸痛哭。

③When he embraced me with his arms open wide, I felt my throat choke with sob.
当他张开双臂拥抱我, 我感觉自己的嗓子哽住了。

④Finally my sister broke down, sobbing into her handkerchief.
我姐姐终于再也控制不住自己的情绪, 捂着手绢呜咽起来。

⑤Neither did I know how I could get through the days a year ago during my fresh year in the company.
在初到公司的那一年, 我也不知道该怎么熬下去。

⑥Her eyes are flooded with tears./Tears are rolling down from her eyes./Tears welled up in her eyes. Eyes begin to water. 她的眼睛充满了泪水。

(三)情景语段

Learning about my father passing way, I felt so sad that I found myself crying unconsciously, unable to hold back my tears. These were miserable days when I feel lonely and extremely exhausted. For a very long time, I could't help myself. And just getting started seems impossible.

二、语篇分析

阅读下面短文,根据内容和所给段落开头语续写两段,使之构成一个完整的短文。

Old Man Donovan was a mean man who hated children. He threw rocks at them and even shot at them with a shotgun. At least that's what we had heard.

His small farm bordered our neighborhood where my younger sister, Leigh Ann, and I lived when we were growing up. His farm was long, narrow, and quaint. It held two treasures. One was his beautiful fruit.

There were many varieties of fruit: pears, apples, and lots more I just can't think of. The fruit naturally drew the children to his land. It made them into thieves. But my sister and I didn't dare to take his fruit because of the horrible rumors we had heard about Old Man Donovan.

One summer day, we were playing in a nearby field. It was time to head back home. My sister and I were feeling very daring that day. There was a shortcut to our house that went through the Donovan farm. We though the wouldn't be able to see us run across his property around the luscious fruit trees. We were almost through the farm when we heard, "Hey, girls, " in a gruff, low voice. We stopped dead in our tracks! There we were, face to face with Old Man Donovan. Our knees were shaking. We had visions of rocks pounding our bodies and bullets piercing our hearts.

"Come here, "he said, reaching up to one of his apple trees. Still shaking, we went over to him. He held out several ripe, juicy, red apples. "Take these home, "he commanded. We took the apples with surprised hearts and ran all the way home. Of course Leigh Ann and I ate the apples.

As time went on, we often went through Old Man Donovan's farm, and he kept on giving us more delicious fruit. One day, we stopped by to see him when he was on his front porch. We talked to him for hours. While he was talking, we realized that we had found the other hidden treasure: the sweet, kind heart hidden behind his gruff voice. Soon, he was one of our favorite people to talk to. Unfortunately, his family never seemed to enjoy our company. They never smiled or welcomed us in.

注意:

1. 续写词数应为 150 左右

2. 请按如下格式在答题卡的相应位置作答

> Every summer, we would visit Mr. Donovan and talk to him.
>
> The next winter, word got around that Old Man had died.

三、文本故事架构

本文属于"人与社会"——"良好的人际关系与社会交往"主题语境。故事的主人公 Old Man 拥有一个水果农场,经常引得孩子们来偷盗,所以他讨厌孩子。然而"我"和妹妹 Ann 在跟 Old Man Donovan 一次接触后,发现他那沙哑生硬的嗓音中"藏"着一颗善良的心。

(一)时空线

故事发生在果园。

One summer day...→as time went on...→one day...→soon 等。

(二)故事情节线

我跟妹妹一起抄近路回家,穿过老人的果园。听闻老人很凶,我们一路小心翼翼,结果就在快要穿过的时候,老人发现了我们。我们感到惊讶的是,老人没有我们预想的那样凶,而是递给我们果子。后来多次经过他家,他依旧给我们果子。我们有一次促膝聊天后,我们发现了他美好的心灵,并成为好朋友。

(三)情感发展线

听说老人很坏(害怕)→一次抄近路,走过老人的农场的时候(胆战心惊)→老人给了我们很多水果(惊喜)→后来多次经过农场,了解老人是一位善良的老人(友好)。情感的变化是从 frightened, surprised 到 friendly。

四、关键信息梳理

(一)人物

语篇出现了 5 个人物,但关键人物是 Old Man 和"我"。

文本中的关键词有：Old Man Donovan，farm，my sister and I，fruit，hidden treasure，kind heart，his family 等。这些词汇在续写故事情节的形成和发展过程中，起着非常重要的作用，抓住了这些关键词就抓住了续写的思路。

（二）提示句分析

从第一段的"Every summer，we would visit Mr. Donouan and talk to him"我们可以推断出，他们经常会在一起聊天。

第二段的"The next winter，word got around that old Man had died"给了我们两个信息。比较明显的就是老人的去世。另外一个较为隐蔽的其实是时间 the next winter。由此我们可以推断出在上一段应该出现一个 one year 的时间点。老人的去世，"我们"去老人的葬礼或者去墓地看望老人，心情很悲伤，或者回想生前跟老人在一起的快乐时光，也可以加入跟老人的家人的互动。

五、写作思路构建

我们每个暑假都去看老人，聊得很开心。随着时间的推移，老人的家人也跟我们熟络起来，对我们的态度也渐渐热情。有一年暑假去看老人，发现老人生病住院，我们去医院看望他希望他早日康复。结果第二年的冬天就收到老人去世的消息，我们去墓地看望老人，带去他看护了一辈子的水果。

（一）习作欣赏

Every summer, we would visit Mr. Donovan and talk to him. He told us different kinds of stories we were fond of. But one summer, we heard that he was hospitalized because he was sick with his throat. Finding out that he was discharged from the hospital, we went over to visit him right away. The family welcomed us. When asked about his illness, they told us not to worry too much. When we were to leave, surprisingly, they offered us some luscious fruit and asked us to visit him as usual.

The next winter, word got around that Old Man had died. Hearing the bad news, my sister and I couldn't hold back our tears. We were heartbroken and decided to go to the funeral. When we arrived, we saw lots of familiar faces from the neighborhood. The family kindly greeted us and said they were so glad we had come. At the moment when we had to say goodbye to Mr. Donovan, our friend, forever, we all wept mournfully, but our wonderful memories of him comforted us. We shall live and pass on his message — to be a man with a kind heart.

（二）习作评价

续写部分用词较为地道，情节简洁紧凑，情感的表达更加生动，"Hearing the bad news, my sister and I couldn't hold back our tears. We were heartbroken and decided to go to the funeral"，痛苦忧伤之情溢于言表。最后的排比句更是把文章情感的抒发推向高潮，并和最后的转折形成一个对比。

第四章 读后续写写作手法运用

第一节 动作描写

动作描写主要用于刻画人物形象,体现故事的生动性。动作描写大量出现在救人、施救、突发情况等主题语篇中。英语中表示动作的动词是动作描写的关键,另外,辅助恰当的形容词、副词或者介词短语,以及各类从句就能更好地体现动作的立体感。动作描写也常常和人物的表情、心理描写相结合。准确细致的动作描写有助于更立体地反映人物的心理和性格特点,使人物形象栩栩如生,跃然纸上。

一、构建语料库

(一)词汇短语

1. 单词

beat	v.敲打;(心脏等)跳动;打败	rise	v.(直)起身;(声音)提高 n.上升;上涨;增长
bend	v.(使)弯曲;屈身	scream	v.& n.尖叫(声);尖叫着发出
bit	v.咬	search	v.搜寻;搜身 n.搜寻;搜查
bow	v.& n.鞠躬;点头	seize	v.抓住
breathe	v.呼吸	sense	n.感官;感觉;意识 v.感觉到
break	v.打破,击破,打断;中断(事物)	shake	v.(使)摇动;握手
catch	v.抓住;接住;偶然撞见	shoulder	n.肩膀 v.承担;担负
chew	v.咀嚼	shout	v.呼喊
cough	v.& n.咳嗽	shut	v.关上;闭上;(使)停止营业
drag	v.拖;拽	sigh	v.& n.叹息;叹气

drop	v.(使)掉下;(使)下降;(使)变弱	sight	n.视力;看见;景象
fetch	v.(去)拿来;(去)取来	slip	v.滑动;滑倒;溜
fill	v.(使)充满;装满	smell	v.闻;闻到
fix	v.固定;安装;修理;安排	sneeze	v.打喷嚏
fold	v.折叠;包;裹	spit	v.吐(唾液、痰等)
grasp	v.抓住;握紧;理解;领会	spot	v.发现;认出
gesture	n.& v.姿势;手势 做手势	stare	v.盯;凝视 n.盯;凝视
hang	v.悬挂;(使)低垂;(被)吊死	strike	v.打;撞击;打动;
hesitate	v.踌躇;犹豫;顾虑	swing	v.& n.摆动;转动
hit	v.敲击;击中	swallow	v.吞下;咽下
hold	v.拿;抱;抓住	taste	v.尝;品尝;尝起来
hug	v.& n.紧抱;拥抱	tap	v.轻拍;轻打
kick	v.& n.踢;踢腿	tear	v.扯(破);(被)撕开
knock	v.& n.敲;打;碰撞	throw	v.抛;扔;猛推
lie	v.平躺;位于;处于某种状态	touch	v.(伸手)触摸;接触(到);触动;感动
lift	v.(被)举起;(被)抬起	tremble	v.& n.颤抖;哆嗦
nod	v.& n.点头;点头同意	turn	v.扭转(身体部位);转动;翻转
note	v.注意;留意	view	n.& v.看;观赏;看待
notice	v.察觉(到);注意(到)	wander	v.漫游;闲逛;走神
press	v.& n.按;压;挤	wake	v.醒;醒来;唤醒
point	v.指出;指向	wave	v.& n.挥手;挥动
pull	v.拉;拖;拔(出);抽(出)	weep	v.流泪;哭泣
push	v.推(动);劝说 n.推;推动	whisper	v.& n.低声讲.低语
raise	v.举起;提高;养育;饲养	whistle	v.吹口哨;鸣笛 n.哨子;口哨
reach	v.伸出(手等);伸手够到;达到	wrestle	v.(与……)摔跤;扭打

2. 词组

a wide smile appeared on her face	面露喜色
absent-minded	心不在焉
arm in arm	臂挽臂地
ask with curiosity	好奇地问
at first sight	一见(就);乍一看
be buried in	埋头于;专心致志于
be filled with fear/anger/happiness	充满恐惧/愤怒/幸福
be lost in thought	陷入深思
bites sb. by the leg	咬住某人的腿
break down	(机器等)出毛病;化合物分解
break in	强行进入,突然进来
break into a run	拔腿就跑
break out	发生,爆炸
breathe/let out a deep sigh	发出深深的叹息
burst into laughter/burst out laughing	放声大笑起来
catch up with	赶上
catch/get/take hold of	抓住;拿着;握住
catch sb. doing sth.	发现某人在做某事
come into view	看得见
come into sight	进入视线;映入眼帘
crash/bump into	撞到
cry her heart out	悲痛欲绝
dash for	冲向
determined eyes	坚定的眼神
drag her legs	拖着疲劳的双腿
eye contact	对视;目光接触
face broaden into a smile	脸上绽放笑容
fall on sth.	目光落在
feel one's way	摸索而行

fix...on/upon	集中(目光、注意力等)于
fold one's arms	交叉双臂
glare at	怒视
give sb. a nod	向某人点了点头
head for	前往
hesitate to do sth.	犹豫做某事
hesitate about/over	对……有所顾虑
hold her head high	高抬着头
hold on(to...)	抓着……不放
hold up	举起;抬起;支撑
hug tightly	紧紧拥抱
in search of	寻找;寻求
knock at/on	敲(门、窗等)
knock down	击倒;撞倒
launch another attack	再次发动袭击
leap/jump/into/off	跳上/跳进/跳下
let go of	放开;松开
let out a cry	大喊
light up	表情眼睛变明亮
lose sight of	看不见;忽略;忘记
lower her head	低头
nod to/at sb.	向某人点头
nod(one's) agreement	点头表示同意
on one's knees	跪着
out of/beyond one's reach	够不到
pull/drag sb. into/onto	把某人拉进/上
pull down	把……往下拉;拆毁
pull out	拉出;拿出
push aside	推开;排挤
quicken her steps	加快脚步

raise her head	抬头
rise to one's feet	站了起来
run away	逃走;逃避
rush/dive/jump into…	冲/跳进去
scream in/with fear	吓着尖叫
search (sth.) for	在……寻找……
shake her head	摇头
she can't take her eyes off sth.	目不转睛
shoulder to shoulder	肩并肩地
shut down	关闭(工厂等)
shut off	关掉;切断
sigh with relief	如释重负地叹气
slide into	偷偷地进入
smile broadly	开怀大笑
speak in a whisper	低声说话
strike sb. as(being)…	给某人……印象
talk to herself	自言自语
tear…into/to pieces	把……撕成碎片
tears spring to her eyes	眼含泪水
throwoneself into his arms	投入怀抱
turn around	转身;转变;好转
turned her head around	转头
turn over	翻身;(使)翻转;翻过(书页)
wake up	醒;叫醒
wave her arms	挥舞手臂
weep her eye's out	大哭
whisper into her eyes	耳语
wipe the tears from her eye's	擦去泪水
within the reach of	在承受的范围内
wraps sb. in one's arms	紧紧抱住某人

（二）话题情景

①She fought him desperately, kicking and biting.

她拼命地跟他搏斗，又踢又咬。

②He dashed along the platform and jumped on the train.

他沿着站台跑着，跳上了火车。

③He stormed out of the room, shutting the door behind him.

他气呼呼地跑出了房间，随手把门摔上了。

④Hardly had Mac stood up when the wolf arrived and was about to launch another attack.

Mac 一站起来，狼就到了，想发起另一次袭击。

⑤Standing there, his lips moved and his eyes were filled with tears with his hands trembling

他站在那儿，嘴唇抖动，眼里含泪，双手颤抖着。

⑥He held up his bicycle and threw it at the wolf, in the hope that the wolf would be frightened away.

他举起自行车朝狼扔去，以此希望狼被吓跑。

⑦Before it could realize what had happened, Paul had already opened the front door and instantly pulled Mac into the car.

没来得及知道发生了什么，Paul 已经打开前门，迅速把 Mac 拽到车内。

（三）情景语段

The champion was just in front of me while John was suffering pain and the lack of hope. Within a mere second, I made the choice, turning around, dashing for John and helping him up. With great surprise and thanks in his wet eyes, John struggled to his feet and ran terribly with my support on his body. Shoulder by shoulder, arm in arm, we managed to hit the end line. In spite of being the last one, we received the warmest applause.

（四）特别注意

●动作描写是反映人物性格和塑造人物特征的手段。动作描写要细致，不要笼统。

①As I came back exhausted, a huge smile spread across her face, which lighted my dull afternoon. (用事物替代人做主语，生动。)

当我精疲力竭地回来时，她脸上洋溢着灿烂的微笑，照亮了我沉闷的下午。

②She danced with delight and passion, thinking nothing, in the achievement of her beauty and in the glory of her success.

女主人开心激情地跳着舞,沉浸在美貌和成功的荣耀之中。

●动作描写多描写动作快、慢和动作的恰如其分。表示动作快,刻不容缓的常用句型:

①hardly(scarcely)had+主语…when 引导时间状语从句(倒装)

No sooner had he got to the lab than he set out to do the experiment.

他一到实验室就开始做实验。

②no sooner had+主语…than 引导时间状语从句(倒装)

I put a note on the door in order that he sees it the moment he comes back.

我在门上给他留了个便条,以便他一回来就能看到。

③as soon as/immediately/the moment/the minute

Hardly had he got to the office when the mobile phone rang.

他一到办公室手机就响了。

●动作立体感强的句子

①We fell hard to the ground and next my gift box flew from my hands and landed on the street with a crash.(本句子通过 fell,flew,landed 三个动词描写物品跌落的过程,又有 with a crash 声音的描述,使句子很有画面感。)

②They sat there anxious. The air froze, and the room seemed darker than it was supposed to be at dusk.(anxious 形容词说明主语的状态。froze 后面使用了比较状语从句。)

二、语篇分析

2017 年 6 月浙江省高考试题

阅读下面材料,根据其内容和所给段落开头语续写两段,使之构成一篇完整的短文。

On a bright, warm July afternoon, Mac Hollan, a primary school teacher, was cycling from his home to Alaska with his friends. One of his friends had stopped to make a bicycle repair, but they had encouraged Mac to carry on, and they would catch up with him soon. As Mac pedaled（骑行）along alone, he thought fondly of his wife and two young daughters at home. He hoped to show them this beautiful place someday.

Then Mac heard quick and loud breathing behind him. "Man, that's a big dog!" he thought. But when he looked to the side, he saw instantly that it wasn't a dog at all, but a wolf, quickly catching up with him.

Mac's heart jumped. He found out his can of bear spray. With one hand on the bars, he fired the spray at the wolf. A bright red cloud enveloped the animal, and to Mac's relief, it fell back, shaking its head. But a minute later, it was by his side again. Then it attacked the back of Mac's bike, tearing open his tent bag. He fired at the wolf a second time, and again, it fell back only to quickly restart the chase.

Mac was pedaling hard now. He waved and yelled at passing cars but was careful not to slow down. He was a steep uphill climb before him. He knew that once he hit the hill, he'd be easy caught up and the wolf's teeth would be tearing into his flesh.

At this moment, Paul and Beeky were driving their car on their way to Alaska. They didn't think much of it when they saw two cyclists repairing their bike on the side of the road. A bit later, they spotted what they, too, assumed was a dog running alongside a man on a bike. As they got closer, they realized that the dog was a wolf. Mac heard a large vehicle behind him. He pulled in front of it as the wolf was catching up fast, just a dozen yards away now.

注意：

1. 续写词数应为 150 左右

2. 请按如下格式在答题卡的相应位置作答

The car abruptly stopped in front of him.

A few minutes later, the other two cyclists arrived.

三、文本故事架构

本文属于"人与自然"——"人与动物"主题语境。主要讲了 Mac 和朋友从家里出发骑行去阿拉斯加，途中遭遇饿狼遇险的故事。在梳理故事情节中，我们要牢牢把握故事发展的三条线，即时空线、故事情节线和情感发展线。

（一）时空线

故事发生的地点是从家骑行去阿拉斯加的途中。

on a bright, warm July afternoon→when he looked to the side...→then...→ at this moment 等。

（二）故事情节线

Mac 和几个朋友从家里骑行去阿拉斯加，途中他的朋友因停下来修理自行车而让 Mac 先行一步。独自骑行的 Mac 被一只"大狗"尾随,之后发现那其实是一只狼。Mac 一边奋力骑行,一边用所携带的喷雾剂驱赶狼,但狼一直紧随其后。更糟糕的是,路过的汽车都未能准确地判断出 Mac 的危险。就在 Mac 快要撞上一处陡坡、看似穷途末路之时,Paul 和 Becky 驾车经过并看到了这只狼,而 Mac 在 Paul 和 Becky 的汽车经过时迅速地把自行车停在了他们的汽车前。

(三)情感发展线

本文应该是以紧张刺激的场景为主。朋友停下修车,Mac 骑车单行(平静)→意识到被"大狗"尾随(一点惊讶)→确定是狼(吃惊)→与狼斗争(恐惧)→过路车求救失败(极度恐惧)→Paul 和 Becky 出现 (充满希望)。

四、关键信息梳理

(一)人物

语篇中有多个人物:Mac,wolf,Paul,Beeky 和 friends。最关键的角色是:Mac,wolf 和 Paul。

文本中的关键词有:Mac, friends, bicycle, pedaled, home, wolf, jumped, cars, climb, Paul 等。Mac 和 wolf 搏斗,是本文最主要的要素,而从所给出的故事情节来看,Paul 和 friends 在救助 Mac 方面起关键作用。bicycle 和 cars,从故事情节来看是关键线索。

(二)提示句分析

根据第一段提示句"The car abruptly stopped in front of him"我们可以推断出,本段重点应该放在 Paul 对 Mac 施救上,同时把动作和心理变化写出来。

根据第二段提示句"A few minutes later, the other two cyclists arrived"我们可以推断出,写作方向应该是 Mac 对施救者的感恩、感激,以及写后来赶到的朋友就刚发生的惊险过程的交流互动,最后完成了旅行。

五、写作思路构建

Mac 挡在车前,Paul 也从刚才的所见所闻中意识到了 Mac 的危险境遇,出于热心对 Mac 伸出援手。Mac 成功获救,之后与朋友汇合。

(一)习作欣赏

The car abruptly stopped in front of him. "Come on, get in the car quickly!" Paul yelled. Without any hesitation, Mac jumped off his bicycle and dashed to the backdoor of the car. It was locked! Thinking of the wolf's bloody mouth, Mac was nearly dead with fright. He could even imagine the wolf's teeth tearing into his flesh. Just at that moment, the door was unlocked and the frightened man dived in, shutting the door behind him. After quite awhile, the disappointed wolf left, disappearing into the woods eventually. Mac stayed in the car, his heart still beating with fear.

A few minutes later, the other two cyclists arrived. They were surprised to find Mac's bicycle lying on the road, his tent bag torn and Mac just like a drowned mouse. Hearing Mac's true story, they sighed in relief, "What a narrow escape!" Mac's friends were also grateful to Paul and Becky. Afraid that there might be more potential dangers ahead, Paul and Becky offered to drive them to Alaska.

（二）习作评价

文中表示紧张、惊恐的心理描写生动反映了主人公所处的危险境地,刻画人物性格栩栩如生。随着故事情节的发展,主人公的危险处境逐渐展现出来。人物的心理描写体现了主人公真实的心理变化,使得 Mac 这个人物形象更为立体丰满。

第二节 细节描写

细节描写通常是指总体描写中,抓住生活中的细微而又具体的典型情节,加以生动细致的描绘,它具体渗透在对人物、景物或场面描写之中。细节,指人物、景物、事件等表现对象的富有特色的细小环节。细节描写在写作中对刻画人物有着非常重要的作用。

一、构建语料库

（一）话题情景

（1）当看到那只凶恶的狼时,我感到很害怕。

At the sight of the fierce wolf, I felt very scared. →（添加合理细节）

①At the sight of the fierce wolf, I felt so scared that my throat tightened and my knees felt weak.（细节描写:嗓子紧,膝盖软）

②At the sight of the fierce wolf, I was seized by a strong sense of horror and my palms were sweating.（细节描写:手心冒汗）

③At the sight of the fierce wolf, I froze with terror, <u>too scared to move an inch.</u> (细节描写:吓得不敢动弹)

(2)一听到那个坏消息,她悲伤不已。Upon hearing the bad news, she felt extremely sad. →(添加合理细节)

①Upon hearing the bad news, her heart ached, <u>tears streaming down her cheeks.</u> (细节描写:眼泪直流)

②Upon hearing the bad news, she, numb with grief, <u>had trouble speaking.</u> (细节描写:不能开口说话)

③Upon hearing the bad news, she felt seized by a burst of sadness and <u>couldn't help crying bitterly.</u> (细节描写:忍不住哭泣)

(二)情景语段

With a pen in my hand, I ran to the testroom in an intense hurry. Endless sweat rolling down my cheeks and wetting my T-shirt, I just had no time to wipe or drink water, for any minute's delay could rob me of the chance to enter the room. Unable to say a single word and out of breath, I managed to make myself stand outside the door of the test room just before the beginning of the exam, which brought out my sign of relief.

二、语篇分析

Rafiki Means Friend

When she was twelve years old, Raha earned a scholarship to study at a boarding school in England. She fondly hugged Mama. She had to say goody to her brown cow, with whom she spent several years. Then Raha and Baba, her father, rode the crowded bus to the airport.

"Your Raha means happiness," Baba said. "Remember that."

As the plane took off, Raha looked out the window at the goat herds and brown rivers of Kenya. She gazed down at the green fields where she used to run like the wind.

At school in England, it wasn't easy for Raha to stay happy.

The teachers gave her dozens of math problems to solve, essays to write, and books to read. Her running coach gave her a striped shirt and white shorts, track shoes and another pair for cross-country. Raha had always run barefoot at home, and the shoes felt tight on her toes. But all the other runners wore shoes, and Raha didn't want to be different.

The team practiced every weekday afternoon. On Saturdays, everyone watched rugby— everyone but Raha. On Saturdays, she ran alone over fields thick with mud. The cold air stung (刺疼) her throat. She missed running barefoot and fast under the hot African sun.

One Saturday, Raha ran up a hill and found herself in a barnyard. One of her classmates named Thomas, stood just inside the barn doors. After he greeted her, Raha asked, "Why aren't you watching rugby?"

"I have to help my father, who is doing stuffs at home down the hill." said Thomas. "Would you like to see the cows?"

Raha entered the barn, and the familiar smell of cows surrounded her. "We also have a cow at home," she said. "I call her Rafiki. That means friend." Raha rubbed the swollen sides of a brown cow. "She'll give birth to a calf (幼崽) soon," said Thomas.

The next Saturday, Raha ran up to Thomas's farm and didn't see him at the barn. Up the hill in the field, she found Thomas's brown cow lying on her side, breathing heavily. "Poor thing, your calf is coming," Raha said. "You need help." She looked out over the fields, but no one in sight.

注意：

1. 续写词数应为 150 左右

2. 请按如下格式在答题卡的相应位置作答

> Raha didn't know how to deliver a calf, but she knew how to run for help.
>
> Looking at the calf, Thomas' father said, "She needs a name."

三、文本故事架构

本文属于"人与社会"——"跨文化沟通"主题语境。文本主要讲了来自肯尼亚 12 岁的 Raha，来到陌生的英国的寄宿学校读书，周末到同学 Thomas 的农场，正碰上奶牛分娩，农场没有人，Raha 及时寻找 Thomas 家人，奶牛平安分娩的故事。考生在阅读这类文本时，应把握故事发展的三条线，即时空线、故事情节线和情感发展线。

（一）时空线

FromKenya to England → One Saturday, Raha ran up a hill in Thomas barnyard→The next Saturday, Raha ran up to Thomas's farm, the cow is giving birth to a calf.

(二)故事情节线

12 岁的 Raha 来自肯尼亚,转到英国的寄宿学读书。初来乍到的她努力适应着周围的一切,但依然怀念在故乡田野上自由奔跑的日子。Raha 热爱跑步,而且喜欢赤着脚跑,可现在却不得不穿着学校发的紧绷绷的鞋子。周六,Raha 在山上的谷仓里意外遇见了同学 Thomas 和他家怀孕的奶牛,这让她想起了自己家的奶牛 Rafiki。第二次看到这头奶牛是在谷仓外的田野,它孤零零地侧躺在草地上,呼吸急促,看起来就要分娩了。但是同学 Thomas 和他爸爸均不在现场,Raha 该怎么办?

(三)情感发展线

从肯尼亚初到英国的寄宿学读书,环境陌生,没有朋友(孤独)→到同学 Thomas 家玩耍(高兴)→在 Thomas 农场看见奶牛分娩,竭力寻找 Thomas 家人帮助奶牛分娩(提供帮助后的快乐)。

四、关键信息梳理

(一)人物

语篇出现了 4 个人物,Raha、Raha 的爸爸,Thomas、Thomas 的爸爸。但关键的人物是 Raha、Thomas 以及 Thomas 的爸爸。

文本中的关键词词有:Cow,happy,run barefoot,Rafiki,friend,help 等。这些词汇在续写故事情节的形成和发展过程中,起着非常重要的作用。抓住了这些关键词就抓住了续写的思路。

(二)提示句分析

根据第一段提示句"Raha didn't know how to deliver a calf,but she knew how to run for help."我们可以推断出,同学 Thomas 和他爸爸均不在现场,看到奶牛就要分娩了,Raha 不知道怎么接生,但她知道求助 Thomas 和其家人。再结合第二段的提示句可知,新生的小牛得到施救。因此,第一段写救援过程,以及 Thomas 和爸爸对 Raha 的感谢。

根据第二段提示句"Looking at the calf,Thomas' father said,'She needs a name.'"我们可以推断出,第二段讲给小牛犊起名的过程,所起的名字应该与文本提供的信息有联系。本段突出了 Raha 在异国他乡有了好朋友以及帮助别人后的兴奋。

五、写作思路构建

Raha 不知道怎么接生,但她知道求助 Thomas 和家人。为了跑的快,Raha 脱掉鞋子,光着脚,像风一样跑去。Thomas 和爸爸及时赶到了奶牛身边,看到新生的牛仔,父子两人很宽慰,感激 Raha。爸爸建议给新生的牛仔起个名。Thomas 建议 Rafiki,并说明原因。

(一)习作欣赏

Raha didn't know how to deliver a calf, but she knew how to run for help. She pulled off her shoes and ran over the fields, barefoot and fast like wind, as she used to run at home, to the place where Thomas lived. When they returned beside the cow in time, a calf was newly born, but it lay weak and still. Thomas's father dragged the calf to the mother's head carefully. The cow smelt her calf, and started to lick its wet fur. The calf opened its eyes and came to herself slowly.

Looking at the calf, Thomas' father said, "She needs a name." After careful consideration, eyes twinkled with excitement, Thomas suggested, "Why not name her Rafiki, just like Raha's cow at home?" Then he smiled at Raha and said, "It means friend." Thomas's father nodded, "That's a good idea! You both make good friends here." It was the first time she felt delighted to be with new friend in the new country. "Baba," she said to herself, "I'm living up to my name. I'm happy to help them."

(二)习作评价

续写部分围绕文章的内容进行了非常合理的续写,紧扣语境,与原文逻辑连接紧密。考生在文中恰当运用了一些高级词汇与句式。特别指出的是,本文的细节描写:"She pulled off her shoes and ran over the fields, barefoot and fast like wind, as she used to run at home, to the place where Thomas lived"和"After careful consideration, eyes twinkled with excitement, Thomas suggested..."增强了语言的表现力,使续写故事更为动人。

第三节　环境描写

故事的发生,情节的展开都是在一定环境中进行的。环境描写在烘托故事情节和刻画人物性格,以及突出语篇主题方面都有很好的作用。

一、构建语料库

（一）词汇短语

1.单词

appreciation	n. 感激;感谢;欣赏	mountainous	adj. 多山的
atmosphere	n. 空气;气氛	phenomenon	n. 现象;奇观
awful	adj. 很坏的;极讨厌的	preserve	v. 保护;保存
bare	adj. 赤裸的;光秃秃的	protection	n. 保护;防护
bite	v. 咬;叮;咬伤 n. 咬伤	rainy	adj. 阴雨的;多雨的
blow	v. (风)吹;刮;打击	renewable	adj. 可再生的;可恢复的
border	n. 国界;边境 v. 与……接壤;与……毗邻	reserve	n. (野生动植物的)保护区
breeze	n. 微风;轻风	rural	adj. 农村的;乡民的
calm	adj. 平静的;镇静的; 无风的	shower	n. 阵雨
camping	n. 露营;野营	sight	n. 视力;看见;景象;情景
changeable	adj. 可变的;易变的	snowstorm	n. 暴风雪
clear	adj. 清楚的;无云(或雾)的	snowy	adj. 下雪的;雪白的
cloudy	adj. 阴云密布的;多云的	species	n. (动植物的)物种;种
cold	adj. 寒冷的;冷的	stormy	adj. 有暴风雨(或暴风雪)的
continent	n. 洲;大陆	storm	n. 暴风雨
damp	adj. 潮湿的;微湿的	survival	n. 幸存;继续生存
destination	n. 目的地;终点	survive	v. 幸存(于);幸免(于);挺过
downpour	n. 倾盆大雨	sustainable	adj. 可持续的;不破坏环境的
foggy	adj. 有雾的;雾茫茫的	terrible	adj. 可怕的;非常讨厌的
fog	n. 雾	threat	n. 构成威胁的人/事物;威胁
freezing	adj. 极冷的;冰冻的	thunder	n. 雷声
frontier	n. 国境;边境	view	n. 视野;风景;观点 v. 看;观赏
geography	n. 地理;地理学	warm	adj. 温暖的;暖和的
hot	adj. 热的;温度高的	warmth	n. 温暖

hurricane	n. 飓风	wet	adj. 潮湿的;湿的
insect	n. 昆虫	wild	adj. 自然生长的;野生的
misty	adj. 多雾的;薄雾笼罩的	wildlife	n. 野生生物
moderate	adj. 适度的;中等的;温和的	windy	adj. 多风的;风大的

2. 词组

a flock of sheep/birds	一群羊(鸟)
a herd of cows/cattle	一群牛(牲畜)
a scenic/beauty spot	风景胜地
come into sight	进入视线;映入眼帘
come into view	看得见
come out	(花)开放;出来
deep blue sky	湛蓝的天空
die out	灭绝;死光;消失
environmentally friendly	环保的
fresh air	新鲜空气
give birth to	生(孩子);引起
give out	发出(光、热、信号等)
global warming	全球变暖
grand/wide/deep/ valley	大峡谷(宽峡谷、深峡谷)
greenhouse effect	温室效应
high/snowed-capped mountains	高山(雪山)
in danger (of)	有(……的)危险
in the wild	在野生环境中;处于野生状态
in turn	依次;反过来;转而
lead to	导致;致使
light rain	小雨
lose sight of	看不见;忽略;忘记
low carbon	低碳的

make a difference	有作用;有影响
pale moonlight	淡淡的月光
pour down	下大雨
running/shallow/deep /stream	流动的河流(浅溪)
spectacular sunrise	壮观的日出
sustainable development	可持续发展
the barking of dogs	狗叫声
the dark,raining evening	漆黑的雨夜
the fragrant flowers	芬芳的花朵
the green grass	绿绿的草地
the perfume of flowers	花朵的清香
thick jungle/forest	密林
warm sunshine	温暖的阳光

(二)话题情景

①The sky was pale with light blue. 天空是一片浅蓝。

②A cool breeze blew through the quiet park.

凉爽的微风吹拂着寂静的公园。

③The wind was perfect for kite flying,bowing just hard enough to give some lift.

今日正是放风筝的好天气,强劲的风力带动了风筝的上升。

④The water was deep blue and sun night glittered on its looking glass-clear surface.

水是深蓝色的,阳光在透明的玻璃表面闪闪发光。

⑤There was a brook not far away from here,rushing between green banks.

离此不远,有一条小溪,在绿色的河岸间奔腾闪耀。

⑥It murmured in a soft voice like a little innocent girl whispering to her loving mother.

似乎它在温柔低语,就像一位天真少女对着她那慈爱的母亲细细私语。

⑦The river makes bends or meanders through low valleys to the plain where rice grows.

小河流蜿蜒地流经低谷,流向生长稻谷的平原。

⑧The moon watched from the sky behind the clouds as the stars blink their eyes in fatigue.

月亮藏在云里,星星略带倦意地眨着眼睛。

⑨Like a dim lamp,the moon shone from above and the stars twinkled their eyes with curiosity.

月亮像一盏昏暗的灯,从上面照下来,星星也好奇地眨着眼。

⑩The moon burst through the clouds and cast its silver lights all over the land.

月亮冲破云层,银色的灯光洒满大地。

(三)情景语段

Tired and hungryJohn finally reached the top of the mountain and a great view unfolded before him. What breathtaking scenery! Endless mountains spread to the bottom of the sky,running rivers made bends between green banks and happy birds flew freely against the sky. The moment he saw this,all the tiredness and hunger were swept up clearly. The efforts were entirely worthwhile.

二、语篇分析

This past summer,my family went on our annual Adirondack vacation on a lake. There are plenty of activities to keep everyone busy:swimming,fishing and sand castle building on the beach. On evenings,everyone gathers on the beach, enjoying themselves.

Anyway, by the third day of our vacation, I had noticed that my sister, Jannie,spent most of her time watching TV and looking through the gift shops in the Internet indoors. She was so attached to her smart phones! At dinner,I told Jannie to enjoy the beautiful wilderness,we should hike to the top of the mountain across the lake the following morning.

"Well,"Jannie answered unwillingly,"Tomorrow there are some games in the the Internet,so I'm going to be pretty busy. ""Come out to enjoy the fresh air and many pleasures, swimming or hiking up mountains!" "Sounds more like punishment than a vacation,"she shrugged(耸肩) her shoulders. "Besides,I don't think I can walk that far. "When I said it only took a half-hour of steady walking to get to the top. She agreed,"Fine,I'll go. "

The next morning was a perfect day for a hike,with sunny clear skies,and the temperature in the low twenty degrees. I got up early and took some sandwiches and water bottles,which I packed into my backpack along with the camera. Jannie came slowly downstairs, announced in a very unenthusiastic, robot-like voice. "I'm ready to go hiking, David. "

Anyway, we stepped out our rented cottage and a quite different view unfolded us. Against the blue skies, a rough path winded to top of the mountain across the lake with wild flowers and grass on both sides. The sunlight brightened on its looking glass clear surface. We began from a path. "I still not sure this is a good idea, but if you could do it, I can too, I guess. "she complained.

注意:

1. 续写的词数应为 150 左右

2. 请按如下格式在答题卡的相应位置作答

> She followed me, absence of mind.
>
> Reaching the top, Jannie opened her eyes wide, shouting：" It's awesome！"

三、文本故事架构

本文属于记叙文,"人与自我"——"健康的生活方式"主题语境。一家人到湖边度假,妹妹 Jannie 躲在房间沉迷于手机,后走出房间,享受自然之美的故事。考生在阅读这类文本时,应把握故事发展的三条线,即时空线、故事情节线和情感发展线。

(一)时空线

度假期间,在湖边别墅妹妹待在室内玩手机、看电视、打游戏,第二天登山。

(二)故事情节线

我们一家人到湖边度假,但是妹妹 Jannie 老是躲在房间沉迷于手机,我想让 Jannie 充分享受大自然的乐趣,邀她一块登山,但她很不愿意,在我的极力劝说下,她勉强同意了。

(三)情感发展线

待在别墅(迷恋手机)→劝说外出活动(拒绝)→开始登山(不情愿)。情感线的发展从 attached to her smart phones, unwillingly, shrugged, unenthusiastic, robot-like voice 这些词汇得到了充分体现。

四、关键信息梳理

(一)人物

语篇出现了 2 个人物,"我"和妹妹 Jannie。

文本中的关键词有："我"和妹妹 Jannie。体现妹妹情感变化的词汇 attached to her smart phones，unwillingly unenthusiastic，robot-like voice 和周围环境自然之美的词汇 a perfect day for a hike，sunny clear skies，the lake with wild flowers and grass on both sides 形成了对比。这些词汇在续写故事情节的形成和发展过程中，起着非常重要的作用。抓住了这些关键词就抓住了续写的思路。

（二）提示句分析

根据第一段提示句"She followed me，absence of mind"我们可以推断出，根据上文内容和续写第一段的开头可知，尽管开始登山了，但 Jannie 心不在焉，故本段可描述 Jannie 和作者在途中的情形，再结合续写第二段开头可知，Jannie 和作者一起到了山顶。

根据第二段提示句"Reaching the top，Jannie opened her eyes wide，shouting：'It's awesome!'"可知，Jannie 被山顶的美景所吸引，故本段应涉及他们在山上欣赏到的景色，Jannie 心里的巨大变化以及行为变化，作者的感受等，描述 Jannie 时可把她的快乐和惊喜展现出来，和前文形成对比。

三、写作思路构建

（一）习作欣赏

She followed me，absence of mind. Minutes later，the road began to climb a steep slope. Jannie sighed dramatically. I pointed out some rarely-seen trees and flowering plants，which I explained were endangered species. She didn't share my enthusiasm. She was thirsty，sweaty and bored. I handed her the water bottle as she sat on a fallen log and took a break. "I missed my screen，" she grumbled as we continued on. Though not happy，she didn't ask to quit before we reached the top.

Reaching the top，Jannie opened her eyes wide，shouting："It's awesome!" The moment her face was shining with indescribably wild joy. A refreshing breeze brushed the mountain top，miles of trees spread out below us. We sat on a large rock and took in the view，while eating sandwiches. "Anyone still wants her phone?" I joked. Jannie rolled her eyes，laughing out. The next morning，Jannie turned up at my door，saying，"Maybe I could go hiking around the lake with you today." "Sure，get our package then，" I replied，relieved and proud.

（二）习作评价

续写部分第一段着重描写了妹妹登山过程中的不愿意的情绪，与第二段看见自然美景高兴的情绪形成了对比,习作中使用了较为丰富的语言和高级的句式。

第四节 性格描写

人物的性格行为是故事类语篇的重要内容。要多角度、全方位地刻画人物,可以凭借把人物的性格跟肖像描写、心理描写、对话描写和行为描写相结合。有的语篇把人物的性格贯穿整个语篇,命题者往往要求考生根据人物的性格发展故事情节。2017 年浙江高考试题就是非常典型的试题。

一、构建语料库

(一)词汇短语

1. 单词

absentminded	adj. 心不在焉的;健忘的	independent	adj. 独立的;自立的
aggressive	adj. 好斗的;有进取心的	intelligent	adj. 聪明的;有才智的
ambitious	adj. 有抱负的;野心勃勃的	mature	adj. 成熟的;(果实)熟的
brave	adj. 勇敢的 v. 勇敢面对	mean	adj. 吝啬的;刻薄的
bright	adj. 聪明的;伶俐的	modest	adj. 谦虚的;适中的
brilliant	adj. 卓越的;才华横溢的	nature	n. 天性;本性
calm	adj.(人)镇静的;沉着的 v.(使)平静	noble	adj. 高贵的;贵族的 n. 贵族
cautious	adj. 十分小心的;谨慎的	optimistic	adj. 乐观的
character	n. 性格;角色(某物的)特色	outgoing	adj. 喜欢社交的;外向的
characteristic	n. 特征;特色 adj. 特有的	personality	n. 个性;人格
confidence	n. 信心;自信	pessimistic	adj. 悲观的
confident	adj. 有信心的;确信的	positive	adj. 正面的;积极乐观的
considerate	adj. 体贴的;考虑周到的	principle	n. 道德准则;准则;原理
courage	n. 勇气;胆量;勇敢	proud	adj. 自负的;骄傲的
courageous	adj. 勇敢的;有胆量的	quarrelsome	adj. 喜欢争吵的
cruel	adj. 残忍的;残酷的	queuejumping	n. 插队

defensive	adj. 戒备的；有戒心的	reasonable	adj. 有道理的；合情理的
demanding	adj. 要求严格的；苛求的	reliable	adj. 可信赖的；可靠的
determination	n. 决定；决心；果断	rigid	adj. 固执的；刻板的
determined	adj. 决意的；坚决的；坚定的	rude	adj. 无礼的；粗鲁的
dignity	n. 尊贵；尊严	self centred	adj. 自我中心的；自私的
diligent	adj. 勤奋的；勤勉的	selfish	adj. 自私的
easygoing	adj. 随和的	shy	adj. 害羞的；羞怯的
enthusiastic	adj.（充满）热情的；热心的	silent	adj. 沉默的；寂静无声的
flexible	adj. 灵活的；柔韧的	simple	adj. 头脑简单的；朴素的
forgetful	adj. 健忘的；不注意的	spit	v. 吐（唾液、痰等）
frank	adj. 坦率的；坦诚的	straightforward	adj. 坦率的
generous	adj. 慷慨的；大方的	strict	adj. 严格的
gentle	adj.（性格）温和的；文雅的	strongminded	adj. 意志坚强的；坚定的
gifted	adj. 有天赋的；有才华的	stubborn	adj. 倔强的；顽强的
greedy	adj. 贪婪的；渴望的	thoughtful	adj. 深思熟虑的；体贴的
hardworking	adj. 辛勤工作的；勤勉的	tough	adj. 严厉的；强硬的；棘手的
hesitation	n. 踌躇；犹豫	warmhearted	adj. 热心肠的；友好的
honest	adj. 诚实的；正直的	wisdom	n. 智慧；明智
humorous	adj. 幽默的；诙谐的	wise	adj. 聪明的；明智的

2. 词组

（be）strict about sth.	对某事很严格
（be）proud to do sth.	做某事感到骄傲
（be）determined to do sth.	决意要做某事
（be）strict with sb.	对某人很严格
a good attitude to/towards life	良好生活态度
a man of principle	有原则的人
be active in（doing）sth.	积极做某事
be considerate to/towards sb.	对某人很体贴

be enthusiastic about(doing) sth.	热衷于某事
be generous to sb.	对某人很慷慨
be honest with sb.	对某人坦诚
be patient with	对……有耐心
be polite to sb.	对某人有礼貌
be responsible for	对……负责
be tough on/with sb.	对某人严厉
by nature	天生地;出于本性地
find fault(with sb./sth.)	挑剔(某人/某物)
gain the courage to do sth.	获得做某事的勇气
good / bad manners	有/不礼貌
in good/bad shape	身体健康/不健康;状态好/不好
it is rude(of sb.) to do sth.	做某事是不礼貌的
keep up/lose courage	鼓足/失去勇气
keep/remain silent	保持沉默
make fun of	取笑
out of shape	变形;身体不健康
play a trick/tricks on sb.	对某人施用诡计/捉弄某人
set an example for/to	给……树立榜样
show/take a(n) attitude	表现出/采取…的态度
swallow one's pride	收起自尊;放下架子
to be honest	老实说
trick sb. into doing sth.	诱骗某人做某事
with great determination and perseverance	有着坚强的意志

(二)话题情景

①She's a very intense person who cares deeply about everything.

她是一个非常热心的人,对每一件事情都极为关切。

②Good listening can really enable us to get close to each other.

善于倾听,让我们走得更近。

③We should value this harmonious relationship between teachers and students.

我们应该珍视师生之间的这种和谐的关系。

④It is working in teams in stead of on my own that has freed me of trouble and made my work more efficient.

是团队合作,而不是孤军奋战,使我摆脱了烦恼,而且工作更有效。

⑤A friendly smile will help you to win others heart.

友好的笑容能帮助你赢得别人的心.

（三）情景语段

My mom is a consideratewoman. Every time I'm done or upset, she can always give me an enormous relief through gentle and warm words. Last month I failed my exam. So sad was I at that time that I threw myself into my room, leaving the door shut behind me, and burst into tears. After a few minutes, mom came in silently, wrapping me by her arms and whispering to comfort and encourage me. With the big support of mom, I picked up my confidence again and progressed more firmly.

二、语篇分析

2017 年 11 月浙江高考试题

阅读下面材料,根据其内容和所给段落开头语续写两段,使之构成一篇完整的短文。

A vacation with my mother

I had an interesting childhood. It was filled with surprises and amusements, all because of my mother—loving, sweet, and yet absent-minded and forgetful. One strange family trip we took when I was eleven tells a lot about her.

My two sets of grandparents lived in Colorado and North Dakota, and my parents decided to spend a few weeks driving to those states and seeing all the sights along the way. As the first day of our trip approached, David, my eight-year-old brother, and I unwillingly said good-bye to all of our friends. Who knew if we'd ever see them again? Finally, the moment of our departure arrived, and we loaded suitcases, books, games, camping equipment, and a tent into the car and bravely drove off. We bravely drove off again two hours later after we'd returned home to get the purse and traveler's checks Mom had forgotten.

David and I were always a little nervous when using gas station bathrooms if Mom was driving while Dad slept："You stand outside the door and play lookout（放哨）while I go, and I'll stand outside the door and play lookout while you go."I had terrible pictures in my mind："Honey, where are the kids？""What？！Oh, Gosh⋯ I thought they were being awfully quiet."We were never actually left behind in a strange city, but we weren't about to take any chances.

On the fourth or fifth night, we had trouble finding a hotel with a vacancy. After driving in vain for some time, Mom suddenly got a great idea：Why didn't we find a house with a likely-looking backyard and ask if we could set up tent there？ David and I became nervous. To our great relief, Dad turned down the idea. Mom never could understand our objections（反对）. If a strange family showed up on her front doorsteps, Mom would have been delighted. She thinks everyone in the world as as nice as she is. We finally found a vacancy in the next town.

注意：

1. 续写词数应为 150 左右

2. 请按如下格式在答题卡的相应位置作答

> The next day we remembered the brand-new tent we had brought with us.
> We drove through several states and saw lots of great sights along the way.

三、文本故事架构

本文属于"人与自我"——"家庭生活"主题语境。主要讲了"我"在孩提时代一次去卡罗莱纳州和北达科他州看望祖父祖母和外祖父外祖母的旅程，"我们"在路上欣赏了美丽的风景，整个过程充满了快乐。这一切，都是因为"我"有一位这样的妈妈：爱心、甜蜜而又心不在焉和健忘。考生在阅读这类文本时，应把握故事发展的三条线，即时空线、故事情节线和情感发展线。

（一）时空线

故事发生的地点是旅行关键点：从家中出发，返回家中，加油站，宾馆。

故事是按时间顺序发展的，旅行的第一天出发了又因落东西回家，在旅途的第四或五晚时，妈妈打算搭帐篷住宿。第二天我们都记起了落在旅馆的帐篷。

（二）故事情节线

我的孩提时代充满了惊奇和快乐，都是我有一位这样的妈妈：爱心、甜蜜而又心不在焉和健忘。假期的时间,我们带上行装,去看望祖父祖母和外公外婆,路上也欣赏美丽的风景,整个过程充满了快乐,而我和哥哥又是提心吊胆,因为妈妈是一个心不在焉和健忘的妈妈。在一个小镇上,我们终于找到了宾馆居住。

（三）情感发展线

旅程出发(不情愿)→返回家中妈妈落东西(有趣)→加油站卫生间轮流放哨(提心吊胆)→找宾馆难,打算在别人家的院子里搭帐篷(善良)→找到宾馆(宽慰)。

四、关键信息梳理

（一）人物

语篇中有多个人物:"我",妈妈,爸爸,哥哥,祖父母,外祖父母等。但是最重要的人物是"我",妈妈,爸爸和哥哥。

文本中的关键词是:absent-minded,forgetful,trip,David,camping,tent,Dad,Mom,nice 等。Mom 是本文整个 trip 的灵魂,她的主要特征是 absent-minded,forgetful。这些关键词都是续写中使用的词汇。

（二）提示句分析

根据第一段提示句"Then next day we remembered the brand-new tent we had brought with us"我们可以推断出,tent 是关键词,由此我们可以推断在第一段中"我们"第一次在旅途中搭帐篷,而根据文章前文提供的主旨,在这一段中可写因妈妈的"健忘"或"善良"而发生的趣事,与首段"filled with surprises and amusements"相呼应。

根据第二段提示句"We drove through several states and saw lots of great sights along the way"我们可以推断出,第一段的结尾事情得到了解决,"我们"继续旅程,这段可描述旅程中所见优美风景,烘托人物愉悦的心情,文章结尾应点题,总的描述这次旅程的趣事以及"我"和哥哥对妈妈的美好情感。

五、写作思路构建

本文首段奠定了故事整体发展基调,这次旅程特点是 strange,interesting。同时,妈妈的性格是文本的最关键信息,续写部分要描写应刻画出妈妈"loving,sweet,yet absent-minded and forgetful"的形象。因此,在后文的续写部分,故事的展开应重点体现妈妈的性格特征。

为了在旅途中体验不一样的感觉,"我们"最终决定搭帐篷,但是当"我们"找到合适的地方时,却发现妈妈把帐篷落在了旅馆,"我们"又不得不回去拿。虽然因为妈妈的健忘,过程波折,但搭帐篷过夜却给了"我们"不一样的体验。在接下去的旅途中,"我们"欣赏了很多美景,因为妈妈健忘的个性,小麻烦接连不断,但却让这次旅行变得更加难忘。

也可以这样设计写作思路:尽管"我"和 David 极力反对,但妈妈坚持要体验住帐篷,结果爸爸同意了。"我们"不得不选择一起搭帐篷,当"我们"顺利搭完帐篷准备睡觉时,却发现妈妈忘了带枕头。第二天早上虽然脖子酸疼,但风景让"我们"觉得一切是值得的。在整个旅途中"我"看到了很多不一样的风景,最终我们顺利地到了爷爷奶奶家。回顾旅程,妈妈给"我们"带来了很多的乐趣。

（一）习作欣赏

The next day we remembered the brand-new tent we had brought with us. Mom suggested that we go camping in the next village, with excitement in her eyes. When we arrived at the camping place, Mom stormed out instantly and urged us to put up the tent. However, she was disappointed to find that it had been left in the hotel! Well, Dad had to go back to fetch it to continue our camping. After finishing the tent, Dad and Mom lay on the grass comfortably in front of the tent with us, talking merrily about the coming plan.

We drove through several states and saw lots of great sights along the way. The bright blue sky, the limitless green grass, the setting sun and the countless stars all kept me spellbound. We also visited my two sets of grandparents. What impressed me most during the trip was that my mom, who was sometimes absent-minded, forgetful, yet always loving and sweet. Every time we got to a new place, Mom would cheer up like a child. She would get off the car excitedly, laughing and dancing around. She was just a big child!

（二）习作评价

妈妈在建议的同时眼里闪烁着兴奋的光芒,这一描写使人物的形象更加的丰满。动词"storm"和"urge"的使用,从动作上更加凸显出妈妈的迫切和兴奋。从人物神情、动作等进行细节刻画,可以使人物形象更加立体化,更具画面感。

第五节　外貌描写

语篇中对人物的外貌特征和服饰的描述,既能展现人物精神风貌,也能呈现出人物心理和思想感情等心理活动,从而塑造出丰满而成功的人物形象。

一、构建语料库

（一）词汇短语

1. 单词

appearance	n. 外观;外貌	neat	adj. (人)爱干净的;仪容整洁的
attract	v. 吸引,引起注意	numb	adj. 失去知觉的;麻木的
attractive	adj. 有吸引力的;有魅力的	ordinary	adj. 普通的;平常的
build	n. 体格;体型;身材	pale	adj. 苍白的
button	n. 纽扣 v. 扣上扣子;(把……)扣紧	plain	adj. 相貌平平的;平常的
casual	adj. 非正式的;随便的	pretty	adj. 漂亮的 adv. 相当;很
confused	adj. 困惑的;糊涂的	roundfaced	adj. 圆脸的
darkskinned	adj. 深肤色的	scar	n. 伤痕;疤痕
dress	n. 衣服;连衣裙 v. (给……)穿衣服;穿……的衣服	serious	adj. 严肃的;认真的
elderly	adj. 较老的;上了年纪的	shoulderlength	adj. (头发)长至肩部的
elegant	adj. 优雅的;雅致的	skinny	adj. 皮包骨的
expression	n. 表情;神色	slim	adj 苗条的
facial	adj. 面部的	smart	adj. 漂亮的;潇洒的
fair	adj. (肤色)白皙的;(头发)浅色的	smooth	adj. 平滑的;平静的;顺利的
fair skinned	adj. 浅肤色的;白皮肤的	straight	adj. (笔)直的;平直的
fashionable	adj. 流行的;时髦的	tense	adj. (神经)紧张的;担心的
feature	n. 面貌的一部分 v. 是……的特征;以……为特色	thick	adj. 厚的;浓密的
figure	n. 体形;身材;人物;人士	thin	adj. 薄的;瘦的,稀疏的
goodlooking	adj. 好看的;漂亮的	thinfaced	adj. 面孔消瘦的
hairstyle	n. 发型;发式	tidy	adj. 整齐的

handsome	adj.（男子）英俊的	tight	adj. 紧的；绷紧的
longhaired	adj. 长发的	ugly	adj. 难看的；丑陋的
medium	adj. 中等的；中间的	wavy	adj.（头发）卷曲的
middleaged	adj. 中年的	weight	n. 重量；体重

2.词组

(be) curious about	对…好奇
(be) of average height	中等个头
…in height	……高
a blank expression/ look	茫然的表情/神色
apply makeup	涂抹化妆品
dress up	（给……）穿上盛装；（给……）乔装打扮
get/have a haircut	去理发
have a good figure	身材好
in one's thirties	在某人三十岁时
in rags	衣衫褴褛
in uniform	穿着制服
judge by appearances	以貌取人
keep/lose one's figure	保持身材/变胖
lose weight/put on weight	减肥/发福；体重增加
wear school uniforms	穿校服

（二）话题情景

①But it was an arresting face, pointed of chin, square of jaw.

那一张脸蛋儿确实迷人得很，下巴颏儿尖尖的，牙床骨儿方方的。

②His friend Mr. Darcy soon drew the attention of the room by his fine, tall person, handsome features, noble manner.

他的朋友达西先生立刻引起全场的注意，因为他身材魁伟，眉清目秀，举止高贵。

③And he was looked at with great admiration for about half the evening, till his manners gave a disgust which turned the tide of his popularity；for he was discovered to be proud；to be above his company，and above being pleased.

人们差不多有半个晚上都带着爱慕的目光看着他。最后人们才发现他为人骄傲，看不起人，巴结不上他，因此对他起了厌恶的感觉，他那众望所归的极盛一时的场面才黯然失色。

④He was a youth eighteen or nineteen years of age，small in stature，with irregular but delicate features.

他是个十八九岁的瘦小青年，面部的轮廓也不大周正，但颇为清秀。

(三)情景语段

He often wears suits and always wears a pair of glasses，which makes him a real gentleman. With his eyes sparkling the light of wisdom，his appearance brings out his rich knowledge. Though he was only of medium height，he was indeed a strong image on the platform. We all noticed his wrinkles spreading around the corner of his eyes，showing his devotion to his teaching career and students.

二、语篇分析

阅读下面短文，根据内容和所给段落开头语续写两段，使之构成一个完整的短文。

A little boy selling magazines for school walked up to a house that people rarely visited. The house was very old and shabby and the owner hardly ever came out. When he did come out，he would not say hello to his neighbors or passers-by but simply just glare at them.

The boy knocked on the door and waited，sweating from fear of the old man. The boy's parents told him to stay away from the house，and a lot of other neighborhood children were told the same thing from their parents.

Dust found the boy lingering on and hesitating what to do. A she was ready to walk away，the door slowly opened. "What do you want?" the old man said impatiently. The little boy was very afraid but he had a quota(份额) to meet for school with selling the magazines. So he got up the courage and said，"Uh，sir，I am selling these magazines and uh，I was wondering if you would like to buy one from me."

The old man just stared at the boy without a word. The boy could see inside the old man's house and saw that he had dog figurines(小雕像) on the fireplace mantle. "Do you collect dogs?" The little boy asked. "Yes，I have many collections in my house. They are my family here and they are all I have." The boy then felt sorry for the man, as it seemed that he was a very lonely soul.

"Well, I do have a magazine here for collectors. It is perfect for you. I also have one about dogs since you like dogs so much. " The old man was ready to close the door on the boy and said, "No, boy. I don't need any magazines of any kind, now goodbye. "

The little boy was sad that he was not going to make his quota with the sale. He was also sad for the old man being so alone in the house that he owned. The boy went home and then had an idea. He had a little dog figurine that he got some years ago from an aunt. The figurine did not mean nearly as much to him since he had a real live dog and a large family.

注意:

1. 续写词数应为 150 左右

2. 请按如下格式在答题卡的相应位置作答

> The little boy headed back down to the old man's house.
>
> From that day on something changed inside the old man.

三、文本故事架构

本文属于"人与社会"——"良好的人际关系与社会交往"主题语境。文章讲述了一个孤独、从不与人打交道的老人,因为一个孩子的小小善举,改变了他的人生态度。考生在阅读这类文本时,应把握故事发展的三条线,即时空线、故事情节线和情感发展线。

(一)时空线

故事发生的地点是街道,老人家中。

A little boy selling magazines for school walked up to a house...→the boy knocked on the door and waited...→she was ready to walkaway...→the old man was ready to close the door...→the boy went home...→the little boy headed back down to the old man's house...→from that day on。

(二)故事情节线

小男孩在卖杂志时来到一位不与周边人打交道的老人家门口。人们都劝他不要靠近老人,小男孩还是敲开了老人的门。老人不愿与小男孩多说一句话,粗鲁地关了门。细心的小男孩观察到老人喜欢狗雕像,他决定把家里的狗雕像送给老人,打消老人的寂寞。文章围绕着小男孩如何通过推销杂志而最后改变老人性格的故事情节展开。

（三）情感发展线

小男孩鼓起勇气向老人推销杂志（害怕）→老人拒绝交流（冷漠）小男孩把狗雕像给老人（同情）→小男孩积极主动帮助老人（感动）。

四、关键信息梳理

（一）人物

语篇中的人物有小男孩和老人。

文本中的关键词有：magazines，the old man，the little boy，dog figurines，lonely 和 real live dog 等。这些词汇在续写故事情节的形成和发展过程中，起着非常重要的作用。抓住了这些关键词就抓住了续写的思路。

（二）提示句分析

从续写第一段首句"The little boy headed back down to the old man's house"的提示，我们可以推断出小男孩应该是带着几年前阿姨送他的那个狗雕像再次去找老人。当小男孩拿出雕像送给老人时，老人被小男孩的行为感动了。

从续写第二段首句"From that day on something changed inside the old man"的提示，我们可以推断出，老人的心理发生了巨大变化。他不再自闭，而是主动与邻居们友好相处，成为一位乐观开朗和积极向上的人。

五、写作思路构建

老人对男孩还是很生气。当看到小男孩把家里的狗雕塑赠送给他时，老人感动流泪，面容瞬间变得温柔和蔼。从此以后，邻居们都吃惊地发现老人不但开始主动和他们打招呼，而且还把家里珍藏的雕像拿出来与孩子们分享。老人被小男孩的善意举动所感化，认识到了生命的价值。

（一）习作欣赏

The boy headed back down to the old man's house. The thought of knocking at the old man's door filled the little boy with fear, though, he still knocked on the door, waiting breathlessly. Finally, it opened, and out came the old man wearing a blank expression. Seeing the boy holding a well-wrapped dog figurine, he looked very astonished but still glared at him without a word. Determined to break the ice, the boy gave the old man the gift with a precious card attached, expressing his care. Deeply moved by all the boy did, the old man could say nothing but to hug him tightly, tears of appreciation welling up. Out of gratitude, he bought a magazine from the boy and saw him off.

From that day on something changed inside the old man. He adopted a real live dog and treated him as his child. It seemed that it was the company of the dog that led the lonely soul out of darkness and loneliness. Gradually, he was willing to greet others with a bright smile, expressing his appreciation to life. Indeed, only when we open up the door of our heart can we be bathed in the brilliant sunshine and enjoy the warmth of love and care.

（二）习作评价

拟人修辞的合理运用增加了语言的感情色彩，分词短语和独立主格的交替使用，使小男孩的各种情绪表达得淋漓尽致，也让老人的感激之情跃然纸上。最后运用倒装结构的说理性总结，升华主题，为整个故事画上了圆满的句号。

第六节　直接引语

记叙文离不开人物语言的描写，尤其是直接引语的使用。恰当地使用直接引语，并添加人物情绪、动作等的描写会使人物形象更加丰满。特别注意的是，读后续写中如果使用过多的直接引语，会破坏故事的连贯性、可读性，因此要恰当使用对话。

一、构建语料库

情景句式

①"Could you possibly loan my father $325," I finished, realizing how absurd it sounded.

"你能借我父亲325美元吗？"话一说完，我就意识到这听起来有多么的荒谬。

②Thank you!" I said in a trembling voice, trying to fight back my tears.

"谢谢！"我声音颤抖地说，强忍眼泪。

③Looking around, he exclaimed, "It's so beautiful here!"

环顾四周，他惊呼："这里好美！"

④"I'll never do that again," he said with tears in his eyes.

他眼含泪水说："我再也不会这样了。"

⑤He shouted angrily, "Give the letter back to me."

他愤怒地大叫:"把信还给我。"

⑥"We won the game!"Jack yelled,his hands trembling with excitement.
Jack 激动地双手颤抖,大喊:"我们赢得比赛啦!"

二、语篇分析

阅读下面短文,根据内容和所给段落开头语续写两段,使之构成一个完整的短文。

I stood on tiptoe and handed the card from my school's help-wanted board to the man behind the counter of Mort's Deli(熟食店). He wore a chef's hat and a clean white apron. Before I opened my mouth,he was shaking his head.

"This is a tough job for any high school kid,"he said. "I need somebody big and strong. "

It was a hard time for my family. As the oldest boy,I was the only one able to help. "Let me work few days,and if you don't like my job,don't pay me. "I said.

He stared at me,then nodded. AtMort's,I worked very hard,washing the dishes. At the close time he called me up. "How much did that card at school say this job ?"he asked. "One dollar an hour,"I murmured.

"That's not enough for someone who works as hard,"Mort said,"You start at $1.25. "

We were closed Sundays,so every Saturday evening Mort urged me to take home the leftover soup in a huge jar. It was a meal in itself,a treat for my struggling family.

My father usually picked me up Saturday after work because the soup was too hard to bring home on my bike. Then one Saturday he let me drive the family car. After work I drove home and parked. With the warm jar in my arms,I passed the living-room window. As I glanced inside,in my father's chair was a large bald(秃顶) man,who was cursing(漫骂) my father. My brothers and sisters sat like statues. Dad's face was stone,and Mom wept.

I crept into the kitchen,set the soup and listened. Dad offered to make the three payments in debt,but the man demanded the entire sum—$325—or the car. I understood how essential a car was. I slipped out,started the engine,thinking angrily. Who might have $325? Who would even consider lending me such a large sum? The only person I could think of was Mort. I drove back to his deli.

注意：

1. 续写词数应为 150 左右
2. 请按如下格式在答题卡的相应位置作答

> The only person I could think of was Mort.
>
> I calmly handed the man the money.

三、文本故事架构

本文属于"人与社会"——"社会服务与人际沟通"主题语境。主要讲了作者"我"的家庭遇到困难时，打工店老板 Mort Robin 慷慨援助的故事。考生在阅读这类文本时，应把握故事发展的三条线，即时空线、故事情节线和情感发展线。

（一）时空线

故事发生在家里以及 Mort Robin 的熟食店。

near the end of the day...→over the next few weeks...→one Saturday after work 等。

（二）故事情节线

初到加利福尼亚，我家经济困难，只能依靠父亲每周几天的工作收入来维持生计。作为家里的长子，我去找兼职为家里分忧。熟食店老板 Mort Robin 一开始拒绝了我，但由于我的坚持，最终留下了我。后来，我通过自己努力工作获得了 Mr. Robin 的认可。Mr. Robin 也经常给我食物救济我家。一个星期六，下班后我回到家发现一个光头男子在我家讨债。他要求父亲一次性归还 325 美元或用车抵债，但在洛杉矶，车对一户人家来说是必不可少的。我溜出家，想办法筹钱。在那时我能想到的只有 Mort。最终我借到了钱，把钱给了那光头男。

（三）情感发展线

求职被 Mort 拒绝时（沮丧）→Mort 愿意给我尝试机会（满怀希望）→后来 Mort 认可我的工作，给我涨薪并救济我家（充满感激）→周六回到家发现父亲被催债时（气愤）。

四、关键信息梳理

（一）人物

语篇出现了 6 个人物，但关键人物是 Mort、"我"、爸爸和光头男。

文本中的关键词有:pay,Mort Robin,the man,my father,car 和 $325 等。这些词汇在续写故事情节的形成和发展过程中,起着非常重要的作用,抓住了这些关键词就抓住了续写的思路。

(二)提示句分析

从第一段首句"The only person I could think of was Mort"的提示,我们可以推断出,"我"准备向 Mort 借钱,但 325 美元是很大的一笔钱,"我"不能确定他会不会借给"我",所以第一段中,"我"提出要借钱时内心应该是有所期待但同时又忐忑、紧张的。

从第二段首句"I calmly handed the man the money"的提示,我们可以推断出,在第一段的结尾 Mort 把钱借给了"我",而在第二段,"我"还了钱解决了家里的燃眉之急。"我"成功地借到了钱,还了债,"我"是高兴的,对 Mort 充满感激的。

五、写作思路构建

(一)思路一

我立即赶往熟食店,告诉 Mort 我家的状况,犹豫着跟他借钱,心里忐忑不安,但令我惊讶的是,他给了我 325 美元,只是说要从我的工资里扣钱。

我向他道谢,然后急忙赶回家。到家后我把钱给光头男子,并要求他离开我家。那一晚我成了家里的英雄,但我知道真正的英雄是 Mort,他不仅将我家从贫穷中解救出来,还提高了我的工资。最终,我把钱还清了。

(二)思路二

我赶往熟食店向 Mort 借钱,在听说了我家的情况后,Mort 很果断地就把钱借给了我。因为担心光头男子威胁我们,Mort 和我一同赶往我家。到家后,我把钱还给了光头男子。他离开后,我告诉家人是 Mort 解救我们于水火之中,我们一家人都十分感激 Mort 并承诺一定会将钱归还。那一晚 Mort 成了我家的英雄。

(三)习作欣赏

The only person I could think of was Mort. Without hesitation I headed for the store in a hurry,knocked at the door and then waited anxiously. After a while, the door opened and there stood Mort, confused. Before he could ask me anything,I poured out what my family was facing. "So,could you possibly loan my father $325" I finished,realizing how absurd it sounded. I could feel my face flushed deeply. Beyond my expectation,he turned around,returned with $325 inan envelope and handed it to me directly,saying"I'll take back half your wages until it's repaid. " "Thank you," I said in a trembling voice, trying to fightback my tears. Then I hurried back home.

I calmly handed the man the money. "Count it, give my father a receipt and get out of our house," I said, a speech I'd rehearsed all the way home. That night I was a hero to my family. But the real hero was Mort Robin, who not only saved us from poverty, but also quietly raised my salary every month. By summer, I was earning ＄2. 50anhour, double the original wage. Finally, I paid off the debt. It was Mr Robin who made the world a better place for me.

(四)习作评价

原文对人物语言的描写较细致,体现出人物当时的状态和情绪。分词状语、介词短语等的添加使得人物的情绪更加的饱满,生动描绘了"我"在说话时的忐忑,还有感激的心情。

第五章 读后续写主题语境

第一节 浓浓亲情 快乐家庭

　　"人与自我"—"生活与学习,做人与做事"主题语境下的"浓浓亲情,快乐家庭"话题是高考重要命题话题。该话题多通过美好家庭的故事来体现,叙述家庭成员之间的快乐、幽默、有趣、和谐相处的关系。山东省2021年高考试题"母亲节给妈妈的惊喜",浙江省的高考题"万圣节雕刻南瓜""健忘妈妈旅游趣事""狗狗与主人"试题都体现了浓浓的亲情和快乐家庭的主题。当然故事里偶有小的摩擦和冲突,有的语篇会涉及主人公和爸爸/妈妈吵架离家出走,后来悔悟的故事;有的语篇涉及主人公迷路的故事;有时会写到兄弟姐妹之间发生冲突,并重归于好的故事,这样的情节是快乐家庭故事的插曲和片段。

一、构建语料库

(一)词汇短语

1. 单词

单词	释义	单词	释义
accompany	v. 陪伴;伴随	loving	adj. 充满爱的
adopt	v. 收养;领养	loyal	adj. 忠诚的;忠实的
affection	n. 影响;感情;喜爱;慈爱	marriage	n. 结婚;婚姻;婚礼
affectionate	adj. 充满感情的;示爱的	marry	v. 娶;嫁;和……结婚
close	adj. 亲密的;靠近的;仔细的 adv. 紧紧地	miss	v. 思念
companion	n. 同伴;伴侣	misunderstand	v. 误解;误会
company	n. 作伴;陪伴	passionate	adj. 有激情的

distant	adj. 疏远的；冷淡的	personality	n. 个性；人格
divorce	n. & v. 离婚；分离	private	adj. 私人（用）的；个人的；秘密的
engaged	adj. 已订婚的；忙于	quarrel	v. & n. 争吵；吵架
excitedly	adv. 激动地	relationship	n. 关系；联系
gently	adv. 轻轻地	respect	n. & v. 尊敬；尊重
gettogether	n. 聚会；联欢会	separate	v. 分居；分手；（使）分离
harmony	n. 和谐；和睦；融洽	shyly	adv. 羞怯地；胆怯地；小心地
host	n. 主人；主持人 v. 主办；主持	silently	adv. 默默地
hostess	n. 女主人；女主持人	simply	adv. 只是，简直
household	n. 一家人；家庭 adj. 家庭的	single	adj. 单身的；单个的
hug	v. 拥抱	softly	adj. 温情的
instantly	adv. 立即	split	v. （使）分裂；（使）分开
kiss	v. 亲吻	treat	v. & n. 对待；款待；医治

2. 词组

be on good terms(with sb.)	（与某人）关系好
break friendship with	与……断交
break up	（关系等）破裂
bring up	抚养；养育
cup one's face in one's hands	双手捂住脸
depend/rely on	依靠；依赖
for company	作伴；陪伴
gave…a long loving hug	长久温情拥抱
get along/on with	相处融洽；生活；进展
go one's separate ways	断绝往来；分道而行
have…in common	（与……）有共同之处
in close relationship with	与……有密切关系
in company with	与……一起

keep in touch(with)	(与……)保持联系
make up	和解
reply softly	轻声回答
share sth. with sb.	与某人分享/合用某物
smile somewhat shyly	有点害羞笑着
split up	离婚;分手;断绝关系
treat sb. like/as sth.	把某人当作……对待
treat sb. to	用……招待某人;以……款待某人

(二)情景句式

①They gave each other a long, loving hug. 他们双方长时间拥抱在一起。

②He gave her an affectionate pat on the shoulder.

他深情地拍了一下她的肩膀。

③Then the man stood up, gazing in the eyes of his oldest son affectionately.

那位男士站在那里,深情凝视着长子。

④The little girl instantly relaxed and simply laid her head on his shoulder, satisfied.

小女孩瞬间放松下来,干脆把头靠在他的肩膀上,心满意足。

⑤He quickly kissed her face all over and then held her close to her chest while rocking her from side to side.

他迅速地吻了吻她的脸,然后把她紧紧地抱在胸前,左右摇晃着她。

⑥Seeing his families sitting together and staying together harmoniously, Cater felt a surge of happiness.

看到他的家人围坐着,和谐地待在一起,Cater 感觉很幸福。

⑦Cheerful singing floating in the room, the two sisters were absorbed in the beauty of the music.

欢快的歌声飘荡在房间里,两姐妹沉浸在音乐的美中。

⑧A wave of happiness and warmth running through her, mom kissed the two sisters gently.

一股幸福与温暖流遍全身,妈妈轻轻地亲了亲两个姐妹。

⑨Approaching Jackson, he gently petted his brother's head, saying, "I'm so sorry for losing my temper."

走近 Jackson,他轻轻地抚摸着弟弟的头,说:"对不起,我发脾气了。"

⑩It was Henry's kindness that made me feel the warmth from our family. I will treasure it with all my heart.

正是 Henry 的善良让我感受到了我们家庭的温暖,我会用心珍惜它的。

二、语篇分析

2021 年 1 月浙江省高考试题

阅读下面短文,根据内容和所给段落开头语续写两段,使之构成一个完整的故事。

Pumpkin（南瓜）carving at Halloween is a family tradition. We visit a local farm every October. In the pumpkin field, I compete with my three brothers and sister to seek out the biggest pumpkin. My dad has a rule that we have to carry our pumpkins back home, and as the eldest child I have an advantage—I carried an 85-pounder back last year.

This year, it was hard to tell whether my prize or the one chosen by my 14-year-old brother, Jason, was the winner. Unfortunately we forgot to weigh them before taking out their insides, but I was determined to prove my point. All of us were hard at work at the kitchen table, with my mom filming the annual event. I'm unsure now why I thought forcing my head inside the pumpkin would settle the matter, but it seemed to make perfect sense at the time.

With the pumpkin resting on the table, hole uppermost, I bent over and pressed my head against the opening. At first I got jammed just above my eyes and then, as I wenton with my task, unwilling to quit, my nose briefly prevented entry. Finally I managed to put my whole head into it, like a cork（软木塞）forced into a bottle. I was able to straighten up with the huge pumpkin resting on my shoulders.

My excitement was short-lived. The pumpkin was heavy. "I'm going to set it down, now," I said, and with Jason helping to support its weight, I bent back over the table to give it somewhere to rest. It was only when I tried to remove my head that I realized getting out was going to be less straightforward than getting in. When I pulled hard, my nose got in the way. I got into a panic as I pressed firmly against the table and moved my head around trying to find the right angle, but it was no use. "I can't get it out!" I shouted, my voice sounding unnaturally loud in the enclosed space.

注意：

1. 续写词数应为 150 左右

2. 请按如下格式在答题卡的相应位置作答

It was five or six minutes though it felt much longer.
The video was posted the Monday before Halloween.

三、文本故事架构

本文属于"人与自我"主题语境下的"浓浓亲情，快乐家庭"话题。作者全家在万圣节雕刻南瓜的家庭故事，叙述家庭成员之间快乐、幽默、有趣、和谐相处的关系。考生在阅读这类文本时，应把握故事发展的三条线，即时空线、故事情节线和情感发展线。

（一）时空线

万圣节前在家里雕刻南瓜。

（二）故事情节线

本文讲述了作者万圣节雕刻南瓜的家庭故事。家里所有人都在厨房的餐桌上忙忙碌碌地雕刻着南瓜，妈妈拿着摄像机拍摄着活动过程。作者将头伸进了南瓜里，被卡住了，无论如何也无法挣脱出来，妈妈却趁机拍下了这一幕，后来作者得救，视频也被上传到网上走红，这段视频开始获得数十万的点击量。

（三）情感发展线

爸爸被喊来帮忙→妈妈拍下了全过程→作者得救→视频被上传→视频走红→视频对作者家和作者的影响。

四、关键信息梳理

（一）人物

语篇出现的人物有：兄弟姐妹、爸爸、妈妈和"我"。

文本中的关键词有："我"是本文主人公，爸爸和妈妈也是非常关键人物。Pumpkin carvin、filming、with the huge pumpkin resting on my shoulders、short-lived 和 can't get it out 这些词汇在续写故事情节的形成和发展过程中，起着非常重要的作用。抓住了这些关键词就抓住了续写的思路。

（二）提示句分析

由第一段提示句"It was five or six minutes though it felt much longer"可

知,第一段可描写作者卡在南瓜中的窘态,自己的努力挣扎摆脱,以及如何在爸爸的帮助下得救的。这一段突出强调摆脱困境的办法以及心理活动。

由第二段提示句"The video was posted the Monday before Halloween"可知,第二段可描写作者头被卡在南瓜里这段视频在网上的走红情况,以及视频走红对作者家和作者的影响。突出浓浓亲情,快乐家庭的主题。

五、写作思路构建

我被卡住后,想尽一切办法挣扎,但都徒劳无功。爸爸被叫来提供实际帮助。妈妈将整个过程拍摄下来,说要将视频上传到Facebook。视频发布后浏览量超过了1000次。人们又要求妈妈把它放在YouTube上,视频获得数十万的浏览量。当我参加青年营时,我被我从未见过的孩子们认出。南瓜也成了小名人。

(一)习作欣赏

It was five or six minutes though it felt much longer. I tied every means to struggle out but in vain. Dad was called in to give practical help. I heard him propose calling the fire department. "Stay tuned," said Mom; she'd mentioned she was going to upload the video to Facebook, but it was only then that I realized she'd been filming the whole time. The video cuts before my rescue —Dad got me to push my head farther into the pumpkin so Mom could reach in and undo the rubber band round my ponytail. I emerged with squash-conditioned hair, a sore chin and my nose plugged with pulp.

The video was posted the Monday before Halloween. By the end of that day, it had over 1,000 views. People asked Mom to put it on YouTube, and by Wednesday morning we were getting 5:00 am calls from TV breakfast shows and then the international media—the video started racking up hundreds of thousands of views. When I went on a youth camp, I was recognized by children I'd never met. The pumpkin also became a minor celebrity. Passersby and trick-or-treaters would knock and ask, "Which is Rachel's pumpkin?" before taking selfies with it.

(二)习作评价

原文对人物语言的描写较细致,体现出人物当时的状态和情绪。"I tied every means to struggle out but in vain" "it was only then that I realized …", emerged、rack up、a minor celebrity 等句型和固定搭配的使用生动描绘了"我"被卡住后的窘境。

第二节 成长故事 反思感悟

"人与自我"—"生活与学习,做人与做事"主题语境下的"成长故事 反思感悟"话题是高考重要命题话题。学生成长过程中会涉及学习、学校生活、同学之间的人际关系。同学之间的相处,会产生令人感动的故事,也难免会产生各种各样的矛盾。成长过程中既有同学间互帮互助,共渡难关的感人故事;也有同学间产生矛盾,重归于好的美好经历。这样的故事多包涵了主人公对已经发生的事情的反思和感悟。

一、构建语料库

(一)词汇短语

1. 单词

absentminded	adj. 心不在焉的;健忘的	patient	adj. 有耐心的;容忍的
awkward	adj. 尴尬的;别扭的	personality	n. 个性;人格
brave	adj. 勇敢的;无畏的 v. 勇敢面对	pessimistic	adj. 悲观的
cautious	adj. 十分小心的;谨慎的	positive	adj. 正面的;积极乐观的;确实的
characteristic	n. 特征;特色	quarrelsome	adj. 喜欢争吵的;好争论的
embarrassed	adj. 尴尬的	queuejumping	n. 插队
hesitation	n. 踌躇;犹豫	regretful	adj. 后悔的;遗憾的
humorous	adj. 幽默的;诙谐的	self centred	adj. 自我中心的;自私的
jealous	adj. 嫉妒的;羡慕的	selfish	adj. 自私的
mean	adj. 吝啬的;刻薄的	sensible	adj. 明智的;合理的;可觉察到的
modest	adj. 谦虚的;适中的	sensitive	adj. 善解人意的;(感情)敏感的
optimistic	adj. 乐观的;抱乐观看法的	thoughtful	adj. 深思熟虑的;体贴的
outgoing	adj. 喜欢社交的;外向的	tough	adj. 严厉的;强硬的;艰苦的
warmhearted	adj. 热心肠的;友好的		

2. 词组

be crazy/mad about	对……着迷;热衷于
be honest with sb.	对某人坦诚
be patient with	对……有耐心
be polite to sb.	对某人有礼貌
be rude to sb.	对某人无礼
be sensitive to sb.	体谅某人
be sensitive to sth.	对某事敏感
be tough on/with sb.	对某人严厉
beyond one's expectations	出乎某人意料地
blame …for (doing) sth.	因(做)……而怪罪……
blame sth. on sb./sth.	把……归咎于……
by nature	天生地;出于本性地
complain (to sb.) about/of	抱怨……
feel sympathy for	同情……
find fault (with sb./sth.)	挑剔(某人/某物)
give up	让;放弃
good manners	有礼貌
hesitate about/over	对……有所顾虑
in high/low spirits	兴高采烈(意志消沉)
in sb's nature	本性如此
in the hope of/in hopes that/in the hope that	怀着……的希望
let sb. down	使失望;辜负
lose heart	灰心
lose one's temper	发脾气
make fun of	取笑;拿……开玩笑
nod with a relief	如释重负地点点头
play a trick/tricks on sb.	对某人施用诡计/捉弄某人
regret doing sth.	后悔做了某事
swallow one's pride	收起自尊;放下架子

tears of joy welling up in her eyes	眼眶涌出高兴的泪水
to sb's regret/delight	让某人遗憾(高兴)的是
trick sb. into doing sth.	诱骗某人做某事

(二)情景句式

①"I wanted to surprise you!" he pointed at a neatly wrapped box with his eyes gleaming.

"我想给你一个惊喜!"他指向一个包装精美的盒子,眼里闪烁着光芒。

②Whenever I thought of Henry's wet book, my face turned red.

每当我想到亨利湿了的书,我的脸都会变红了。

③Then I gave him a big hug and tears of gratitude welled up in my eyes.

然后我给了他一个大大的拥抱,感激的泪水在我眼里涌出。

④Deeply touched by his kindness, I felt my blood rush to face.

我被他的善良深深感动,我觉得我的脸变得很红。

⑤If I had followed and hadn't quarreled with Tom, I wouldn't have got lost.

如果我听 Tom 的,不跟他吵架,我也不会迷路。

二、语篇分析

2021 年浙江省高考试题

阅读下面短文,根据内容和所给段落开头语续写两段,使之构成一个完整的短文。

My dad, George, only had an eighth grade education. A quiet man, he did't understand my world of school activities. From age 14, he worked. And his dad, Albert, took the money my dad earned and used it to pay family expenses.

I didn't really understand his world either: He was a livestock trucker, and I thought that I would surpass(超过)anything he had accomplished by the time I walked across the stage at high school graduation.

Summers in the mid-70s were spent at home shooting baskets, hitting a baseball, or throwing a football, preparing for my future as a quarterback on a football team. In poor weather, I read about sports or practiced my trombone(长号).

The summer before my eighth grade I was one of a group of boys that a neighboring farmer hired to work in his field. He explained our basic task, the tractor fired up and we were off, riding down the field looking for weeds to spray with chemicals. After a short way, the farmer stopped and pointed at a weed which we missed. Then we began again. This happened over and over, but we soon learned to identify different grasses like cockleburs, lamb's-quarters, foxtails, and the king of weeds, the pretty purple thistle. It was tiring work, but I looked forward to the pay, even though I wasn't sure how much it would amount to.

At home, my dad said, "A job's a big step to growing up. I'm glad you will be contributing to the household." My dad's words made me realize that my earnings might not be mine to do with as I wished.

My labors lasted about two weeks, and the farmer said there might be more work, but I wasn't interested. I decided it was not fair that I had to contribute my money.

注意：

1. 续写词数应为 150 左右

2. 请按如下格式在答题卡的相应位置作答

The pay arrived at last.

I understood immediately what my parents were worried about.

三、文本故事架构

本文属于"人与自我"主题语境下的"成长故事 感悟反思"话题。文章讲述了作者高中毕业后,参加农场工作,辛辛苦苦挣到的钱,不情愿贡献给家庭,后来在看到父亲的辛劳之后,理解了父母担心的是自己太过自私而不知奉献,终于想通,并自豪地将自己劳动所得交给父亲的故事。考生在阅读这类文本时,应把握故事发展的三条线,即时空线、故事情节线和情感发展线。

（一）时空线

暑假在农场劳动了两周,领工资回家面对父亲。

（二）故事情节线

父亲是个卡车司机,只有八年级的教育水平,他是一个很安静的人,不懂得我在学校的生活。我认为我八年级的时候能够超越他。八年级前的暑假,我到邻居家的农场干活。劳动确实非常艰苦,我盼望着得到我的工资。十多天的劳动,我能拿多少的工资呢？回到家,爸爸说,工作是成长的一大步。劳动了两周,农场主说还有更多的活可以干,但是我没有兴趣,我只关心我能挣多少钱。

（三）情感发展线

农场劳动(辛苦)→计划自己消费(兴奋)→父亲希望我的工资为家庭贡献(不情愿)→盼望领到工资(着急)→领到工资(兴奋)→把工资交给父亲(自豪)。

四、关键信息梳理

（一）人物

语篇出现了2个人物，"我"和父亲。

文本中的关键词有："我"是本文主人公，"父亲"也是非常关键的人物。tiring，worked growing up，family，realized，farmer，learned，my parents 和 fair 这些词汇在续写故事情节的形成和发展过程中，起着非常重要的作用。抓住了这些关键词就抓住了续写的思路。

（二）提示句分析

根据第一段提示句"The pay arrived at last"我们可以推断出，第一段可描写作者的工资到手后，高兴地计划自己用这笔钱，不愿意交给父亲，然后看到父亲的辛劳。要把"我"的心理活动写出来。

根据第二段提示句"I understood immediately what my parents were worried about"我们可以推断出，第二段可描写作者明白了父母担心自己不懂得奉献，想通了，然后自豪地把钱交给了父亲。

五、写作思路构建

工资终于发下来了。我非常高兴我拿到了的劳动所得！暂且忘记了劳动的艰苦，我在计划着怎样花这部分钱。回到家，爸爸问我发了多少钱，我不愿意透露。爸爸第二天劳动的情景，深深地留在我的脑海中，我又想起了爸爸那句话，工作是成长的一大步。我立刻明白了父母所担心的，他们担心我太自私，不会给予和奉献，我意识到了劳动的辛苦，我的成长和整个家庭的幸福都离不开父母艰辛的劳动。于是最后我把钱交给了爸爸。

（一）习作欣赏

The pay arrived at last. Although the job was very tiring, I was very happy in my heart for I got something from my work. The toil of labor was forgotten for the time being. I thought I should have my own money and planned how to spend it. "How much money have you earned?" Dad asked. I was surprised, reluctant to say my income. The next morning, my dad's livestock truck started running. I saw my father's hard‑working figure and thought of his words "A job's a big step to growing up".

I understood immediately what my parents were worried about. They were worried that I was too selfish to give. I realized that my labor was very hard, but my growth and our whole family had been depending on the hard work of my parents! Dad never complained about unfairness! He even seemed to think that was fair. I thought, "I've only worked for two weeks, but how many years my father has worked!" In the evening, Dad came back. I proudly took out my own money and handed it to Dad.

(二)习作评价

本文思路清晰,续写的两段与原文融洽度高,优秀句式结构和高级词汇多。"I thought I should have my own money and planned how to spend it"运用了疑问词加动词不定式作宾语。"I realized that my labor was very hard, but my growth and our whole family had"使用了宾语从句以及过去完成进行时。

第三节 助人为乐 丰富人生

"人与社会"—"社会服务与人际沟通"主题语境下的"助人为乐 丰富人生"话题是高考读后续写命题常见话题。助人为乐话题体现在同学、邻里以及陌生人之间互帮互助,雪中送炭。这一话题常常体现了救助者善良、同情的朴素的情感,也包含了被救助者的感恩感激之情。2020 年全国新高考 I 卷读后续写试题就是这类话题:Meredith 和孩子想出了一个主意——制作爆米花,让家庭贫困的 Bernard 去卖爆米花,从而帮助了 Bernard 一家摆脱困境的故事。

一、构建语料库

(一)词汇短语

1. 单词

assist	v. 帮助;协助	eager	adj. 渴望的;热切的
assistance	n. 帮助;协助;援助	urge	v. 催促;力劝;极力主张 n. 强烈的冲动

2.词组

(be) eager to do sth.	渴望做某事
be crazy/mad about	对……着迷；热衷于
be enthusiastic about (doing) sth.	对(做)某事很有热情
be fond of	喜爱；爱好
be thankful for	感激……
do sb. a favour	帮某人一个忙
in return (for sth.)	作为(……的)交换；作为(……的)回报
owe sb. sth./owe sth. to sb.	应该给某人某物/欠某人某物
persuade sb. into (doing) sth.	说服某人(做)某事
with the help of	在某人的帮助下；借助某人

(二)情景句式

①But for Henry's help, I wouldn't have finished my performance smoothly.

如果没有 Henry 的帮助，我就不会顺利地完成我的演出了。

②I sincerely thanked them for their kind help.

我真诚地感谢他们善意的帮助。

③They were deeply moved, especially Bernard, who finally found a way to make money for his family.

他们被深深地感动了，特别是 Bernard 帮助这一家人筹集到了钱。

④Arriving home, I wrote to him and his wife a thank-you note for helping me.

因为帮了我，一到家，我就给他和他的妻子写了一封感谢信。

⑤I was definitely grateful to her for extending a helping hand.

我非常感激她伸出援手。

⑥It was Ryan's timely assistance that made me avoid the embarrassment. I am proud to have such a selfless and kind friend.

正是 Ryan 的及时帮助使我避免了尴尬。我很自豪能有这样一个无私善良的朋友。

⑦If it wasn't Dad's help, we couldn't finish it.

要不是爸爸的帮助，我们就无法完成。

⑧As I was about to give up,Tom came to his help.

我正要放弃的时候,Tom 过来帮助。

二、语篇分析

2020 年 7 月新高考卷

阅读下面材料,根据其内容和所给段落开头语续写两段,使之构成一篇完整的短文。

The Meredith family lived in a small community. As the economy was in decline,some people in the town had lost their jobs. Many of their families were struggling to make ends meet. People were trying to help each other meet the challenges.

Mrs. Meredith was a most kind and thoughtful woman. She spent a great deal of time visiting the poor. She knew they had problems,and they needed all kinds of help. When she had time,she would bring food and medicine to them.

One morning she told her children about a family she had visited the day before. There was a man sick in bed,his wife,who took care of him and could not go out to work,and their little boy. The little boy ——his name was Bernard——had interested her very much.

"I wish you could see him," she said to her own children,John,Harry,and Clara. "He is such a help to his mother. He wants very much to earn some money,but I don't see what he can do. "

After their mother left the room,the children sat thinking about Bernard. "I wish we could help him to earn money. "said Clara. "His family is suffering so much. "

"So do I," said Harry. "We really should do something to assist them. "

For some moments, John said nothing, but, suddenly, he sprang to his feet and cried, "I have a great idea! I have a solution that we can all help accomplish (完成). "

The other children also jumped up all attention. When John had an idea, it was sure to be a good one. "I tell you what we can do," said John. "You know that big box of corn Uncle John sent us? Well,we can make popcorn(爆米花), and put it into paper bags, and Bernard can take it around to the houses and sell it. "

注意:

1. 续写词数应为 150 左右
2. 请按如下格式在答题卡的相应位置作答

> When Mrs. Meredith heard of John's idea, she thought it was a good one, too.
>
> With everything ready, Bernard startedout on his new business.

三、文本故事架构

本语篇属于"人与社会"—"做人与做事"主题语境下的"助人为乐 丰富人生"话题。文本主要讲述的是,在妈妈的启示下,三个孩子在有限的条件下,帮助另外一个想要帮助父母维持生活的小男孩的动人故事。考生在阅读这类文本时,应把握故事发展的三条线,即时空线、故事情节线和情感发展线。

(一)时空线

这是在经济大萧条时期,在一个小社区发生的感人故事。

The period when the economy was in decline in a small community→One morning she told her children→After their mother left the room→For some moments→Suddenly, John had an idea→When Mrs. Meredith heard of John's idea →With everything ready 等。

(二)故事情节线

在社会经济萧条的环境下,妈妈 Mrs. Meredith 一直乐于助人。一个充满爱心的妈妈,身体力行,在三个孩子心中播种了爱和善良的种子。她给孩子们讲述了 Bernard 一家的困境后,三个孩子 John, Harry 和 Clara 非常渴望帮助 Bernard,并且确实想出了一个好主意,即把家里的玉米做成爆米花,让 Bernard 在社区售卖。

(三)情感发展线

善良体贴的 Mrs. Meredith 经常拜访贫民区,接济穷苦人(同情、善良)。→妈妈把见到的穷苦的 Bernard 家的故事分享给三个孩子,打算帮助 Bernard 一家(共鸣)。→孩子们冥思苦想,John 有了好办法:把家里的玉米做成爆米花,让 Bernard 在社区售卖(竭尽全力)。本文的情感发展线是:听到故事→产生共鸣→表示同情→想出方法→立即行动。

四、关键信息梳理

（一）人物

语篇中的人物看起来很多：Mrs. Meredith，三个孩子 John、Harry 和 Clara，穷苦的男孩 Bernard 和生病的爸爸以及照顾爸爸的妈妈。但关键的人物应该是 Mrs. Meredith，三个孩子和被救助的孩子 Bernard。

文本中的关键词有：Mrs. Meredith，Bernard，kind，assist，idea，popcorn 和 sell。这些词汇在续写故事情节的形成和发展过程中，起着非常重要的作用，抓住了这些关键词就抓住了续写的思路。

（二）提示句分析

根据第一段提示句"When Mrs. Meredith heard of John's idea, she thought it was a good one, too"我们可以推断出，John 说出了自己的想法，妈妈同意 John 的观点，认为是一个好主意。本段主要写这个想法的好处，以及为实施这个方案的各种准备工作。

根据第二段提示句"With everything ready, Bernard started out on his new business"我们可以推断出，三个孩子分头行动，开始爆玉米花。男孩 Bernard 卖爆米花的成功，之后两家人和谐相处以及和情谊的延续。

五、写作思路构建

Meredith 乐于帮助，而 Bernard 需要帮助。Mrs. Meredith 家的三个孩子集思广益，John 想出救助 Bernard 男孩一家的方案，大家都觉得好，而妈妈听了 John 的想法，也觉得是好办法。孩子们对这一方案充满期待。等到准备工作完成，孩子们立即行动，开始爆玉米花。开始并不顺利，逐渐摸索出爆米花的规律。男孩 Bernard 在街道卖爆米花，确实挣的钱多了，增加了家庭收入，爸爸的病也逐渐好转。Bernard 一家感激孩子们的帮助。

也可以这样设计写作思路：

Meredith 乐于帮助，而 Bernard 需要帮助。Mrs. Meredith 的三个孩子集思广益，John 想出救助 Bernard 男孩一家的方案，大家都觉得好，而妈妈听了 John 的想法，也觉得是好办法。妈妈就和孩子们讨论这一方案，并不断完善，孩子们对这一方案充满期待。准备工作完成，孩子们立即行动，开始爆玉米花。爆米花的善良故事在小区传播，人们纷纷来买男孩 Bernard 的爆米花，这增加了 Bernard 一家的家庭收入，爸爸有了治病的钱，很快恢复了健康，Bernard 一家感激孩子们的帮助。

（一）习作欣赏

When Mrs. Meredith heard of John's idea, she thought it was a good one, too. She nodded with a smile and encouraged the children, "Let's get started!" Immediately, Clara volunteered to get the big box of corn and prepared the microwave oven to make popcorn. At the same time, John went to purchase some paper bags and arranged all the stuff in place. Harry ran to Bernard's and dragged him to the scene. After hearing the explanation, Bernard was overwhelmed with excitement and gratitude. They can hardly wait. Time went by swiftly, and the children laughed, carrying out their great "project". Joy filled the yard and everyone's heart.

With everything ready, Bernard started out on his new business. Carrying all the paper bags, he called out, "Popcorn! 50 cents for one extra‐large pack!" People started to gather around him, which drew even more people. Everyone was ready to buy one pack to support him. The air was rich with happiness and kindness. Within no time, Bernard sold out all popcorn and earned quite some money. On returning, he thanked the Meredith family with watery eyes. For Clara, Harry and John, it was an unforgettable experience as well. It turned out that their efforts not only helped a brother in need, but also gave themselves the sweet taste of helping others.

（二）习作评价

"She nodded with a smile and encouraged the children, 'Let's get started!'"体现了妈妈教育孩子帮助他人的人物形象。接下来的准备爆米花的动作很形象，动词的使用很得体。Bernard 感恩之情溢于言表，最后一句话升华了主题。

第四节　优秀品行　美丽人生

"优秀品行 美丽人生"是"人与自我"—"生活与学习，做人与做事"主题语境下的话题。

学生的优秀品质是读后续写话题所涉及的重要内容，其包括以下方面：宽容大度，合作共处；不畏挫折，自强不息；乐观开朗，积极向上，有错就改；拾金不昧，诚实守信；言行一致，不说谎不作弊；主动分担家务，自强自律等。

一、构建语料库

(一)词汇短语

1.单词

ability	n.能力；才能	dilemma	n.进退两难；窘境；困境
aggressive	adj.好斗的；有进取心的	disadvantage	n.不利；不利条件；缺点
ambitious	adj.有抱负的；野心勃勃的	dive	v. & n.跳水；俯冲；全身心投入
appreciate	v.感激；欣赏；赏识；理解	downtoearth	adj.脚踏实地的
attempt	n. & v.试图；尝试；努力	effort	n.努力；尽力
attitude	n.态度；看法	encourage	v.鼓励；激励
capable	adj.有能力的；能干的	flexible	adj.可变通的；灵活的
challenge	n.挑战(赛)；挑战 v.向……挑战	generous	adj.慷慨的；大方的
competent	adj.合格的；能干的；胜任的	gentle	adj.(性格)温和的；文雅的
confidence	n.信心；自信；信赖	hardship	n.苦难；困苦；苦事
confident	adj.有信心的；自信的；确信的	honour	n.荣誉；尊敬；敬意
cooperate	v.合作；协作；配合	intelligent	adj.聪明的；有才智的；有智力的
courage	n.勇气；胆量；勇敢	personality	n.个性；人格
courageous	adj.勇敢的；有胆量的	strongminded	adj.意志坚强的；坚定的
deserve	v.应受；值得	weakness	n.弱点；缺点
determination	n.决定；决心；果断	will	n.意志；决心
determined	adj.决意的；坚决的；坚定的	worthwhile	adj.值得花时间/精力的
difficulty	n.困难；难事		

2. 词组

(be)determined to do sth.	决意要做某事
a good attitude to/towards life	良好的生活态度
ability to do sth.	做某事的能力
accept/take up the challenge	接受挑战
achieve/attain/gain honour	获得荣誉
admit/accept defeat	承认失败
against one's will	违背某人的意愿
allround development	全面发展
at a disadvantage	处于不利地位
be buried in/bury oneself/one's face(head etc.)in	埋头于;专心致志于
be generous to sb.	对某人很慷慨
come to one's aid	帮助某人
end up	结束;告终
fight for	为……而战
focus…on	集中……于
give in	屈服;让步
give up	让;放弃
go through	穿过;经历
have difficulty (in) doing sth.	做某事有困难
in an attempt to	为了
keep up/lose courage	鼓足/失去勇气
leave/make an impression on sb.	给某人留下印象
lose heart	灰心
make every effort to	尽一切努力
make excuses for	为……找借口
make it	做到;成功;准时到达
make progress	取得进步
make up one's mind	作出决定;下定决心
overcome difficulties	克服困难

owe sb. sth.	应该给某人某物/欠某人某物
owe…to	把……归功于
pay off	取得成功;得到好结果
persuade sb. to do sth.	说服某人做某事
put effort into	把精力放在……
put up with	忍受;容忍
remind sb. of sb./sth.	使某人想起某人/某事
run into difficulties	遇到困难
show/take a(n) attitude	表现出/采取……的态度
spare no effort to do sth.	不遗余力做某事
stick to	坚持;遵守
take pains to do sth.	努力/下苦功做某事
to the best of one's ability	尽最大努力
turn out	原来(是);证明(是);结果(是)
win the respect of	赢得……的尊重

(二)情景句式

①Courage is the the most important quality that I wanted her to possess.

勇敢是我想让她拥有的最重要的品质。

②Igathered the courage to take the first step onto the suspension bridge, then another,I inched forward,all the way holding on tight to the handrail.

我鼓起勇气在悬索桥上迈出第一步,之后,一步步小心翼翼向前走,紧紧抓住栏杆。

③I knew for sure that every time I lost patience in the future I would always remember my grandfather's words.

我确信,将来每当我失去耐心时,我都会记住祖父的话。

二、语篇分析

山东潍坊模考试题

阅读下面材料,根据其内容和所给段落开头语续写两段,使之构成一篇完整的短文。

An honest mistake

Karie double-checked the words on her spelling test. If she got 100 percent today, she'd win her class' First-Quarter Spelling Challenge and a brand-new dictionary. Plus, Ms. McCormack had promised to do a handstand if anyone got a perfect score.

Three more words to go. N-i-c-e-l-y. Q-u-i-c-k-l-y. H-o-n-e-s-t-y. Wait! She'd spelled honesly, not hones. She erased the t-y and wrote l-y before handing in her paper.

Ms. McCormack graded the test papers at the break. Meanwhile, Karie sat restlessly in her seat with her fingers crossed. Ms. McCormack walked to the front of the room and cleared her throat. Then, as if she were an Olympic gymnast, Ms. McCormack's feet flipped into the air.

"Congratulations, Karie! You did it!" she announced while upside down.

The whole class burst into applause! Ms. McCormack righted herself and presented Karie with her prize. Karie grinned as she read the label on the box:

To Karie Carter, for her perfect first-quarter score in spelling.

"Everything OK?" Mom asked as Karie burst through the front door after school. Karie didn't answer. As if by magic, she took out her spelling test and prize and showed them to her mother. Mom hugged her, asking her to put the test paper on the fridge so that Dad could see it when he got home.

Karie took another look at the test paper before putting it on the fridge. Her hands stopped in the mid air. She just couldn't believe her own eyes. Honesly?

YES! H-O-N-E-S-L-Y!

Mom sensed something unusual and asked why. Karie stuffed the test paper into her backpack and explained that she was justtoo excited. Mom brought her some tea. Yes, a "t" was exactly what she needed.

After drinking a few sips, Karie plodded(重步走) down the hall, lost in thought. Father promised they would celebrate it tonight if she could win the contest. And how could she tell the class she hadn't earned the prize after all? That Ms. McCormack did the handstand for nothing?

注意：

1. 续写词数应为 150 左右

2. 请按如下格式在答题卡的相应位置作答

> Soon Father came back with excitement.
>
> The next morning, Karie went to school earlier than usual.

三、文本故事架构

本文属于"人与自我"——"生活与学习 做人与做事"主题语境下的 "优秀品行 美丽人生"话题。文章记叙了 Karie 女孩参加"拼写大赛"被宣布 为获胜者后，自己发现错误，主动上交奖品的故事，文章突出了 Karie 女孩诚 实的优秀品质。考生在阅读这类文本时，应把握故事发展的三条线，即时空 线、故事情节线和情感发展线

（一）时空线

故事发生在学校和家里。

（二）故事情节线

Karie 女孩参加"第一季度拼写大赛"，老师 Ms. McCormack 允诺，会做倒 立的空手翻动作为胜者祝贺，并颁发奖品。眼看胜利在望，Karie 却在最后时 刻把 Honesty 写成了 Honesly。老师 Ms. McCormack 评定分数时没有看出错 误，看到结果后，立即做出倒立的空手翻动作，宣布 Karie 完美获胜并颁发奖 品，班内掌声雷动！Karie 抚摸奖品心情无比激动。

回家妈妈问询，Karie 自豪拿出奖品和试卷给妈妈看，妈妈激动地拥抱女 儿，并嘱咐把完美试卷贴在爸爸看得见的电冰箱上。Karie 拿出试卷刚要张 贴，发现 Honesty 写错了。妈妈意识到了不对劲，忙问为什么，Karie 说不太 好受。妈妈揉揉女儿的背，安慰说可能太激动的原因。妈妈说，"来点茶？" Karie 呷了小口茶，Karie 拖着沉重的脚步走过客厅，沉思着。爸爸回家要庆 祝她的获胜，回校后又怎样面对同学呢？

（三）情感发展线

Karie 参加拼写大赛获胜（无比激动）→回家妈妈激动地拥抱女儿（自豪 幸福）→Karie 拿出试卷要张贴，发现 Honesty 写错了（愧疚难受）→面对爸爸 （说明原因主动）。

四、关键信息梳理

（一）人物

语篇出现的人物有 Karie、妈妈、爸爸、老师 Ms. McCormack。

文本中的关键词有 Honesty，prize，a brand-new dictionary，the test paper，excitement 等，这些词汇在续写故事情节的形成和发展过程中，起着非常重要的作用。抓住了这些关键词就抓住了续写的思路。

（二）提示句分析

根据第一段提示句"Soon Father came back with excitement"我们可以推断出，爸爸急切地想看看女儿的奖品，并打算好好庆贺，要和 Karie 的愧疚心理活动形成对比。

根据第二段提示句"The next morning, Karie went to school earlier than usual"我们可以推断出，Karie 主动说明错误并上交奖品突出诚实的主题。

五、写作思路构建

标题 An honest mistake 反映了故事的主题，这就给我们的续写提供了方向和思路。写作思路可这样构建：

爸爸回来了，激动地说，"我要看看你的试卷和奖品！"可是 Karie 手里攥着试卷，心情非常沉重，毕竟是因为自己的粗心而失去了这场竞赛的胜利！了解到了整个故事，爸爸拥抱了女儿，"我仍然为你骄傲！"第二天早上带着试卷和奖品，她早早地来到了学校，勇敢地走向老师的办公室，她认真地跟老师说明了情况，并上交了奖品。老师又把奖品给了她，说奖品应该给她，因为她的诚实而获奖！

（一）习作欣赏

<u>Soon Father came back with excitement.</u> "Have a look at your test paper, Karie!" Dad said in an eager and excited tone. However, Karie froze there with the test paper in her hand, tears rolling down her checks. Anyhow, it was a struggle for he to accept the fact that she failed the contest due to her last carelessness. Worst till, she was announced the winner and received the thunderous applause of the whole class! knowing the whole story, father hugged her with his arms open wide, "I'm also proud of you, sweetie." A warm current rose in Karie's heart.

<u>The next morning, Karie went to school earlier than usual.</u> With the paper and the dictionary, she bravely went over to Ms. McCormack, who was preparing

her lessons at desk. She was wondering what was the matter when Karie said, "I misspelled honestly and you didn't catch it. I can't keep this." For a moment, Ms. McCormack stood quietly reading the label on the dictionary. Then she picked up her pen, crossed out the initial word Perfect and wrote Honest before handing the dictionary back to Karie. "Keep this. But for honesty."

(二)习作评价

续写部分思路清晰，与文本的融洽度高。使用了很多优秀的句子结构，in an eager and excited tone, froze there with the test paper in her hand, tears rolling down her checks 以及 bravely 等，突出了情感表达。

第五节 友情友谊 包容合作

"人与社会"—"社会服务与人际沟通"以及"人与自我"—"生活与学习，做人与做事"主题语境都涉及友情友谊，而友谊友情是读后续写的重要话题之一。对于青春期的学生来讲友谊是一份特别的期许，牢固不破的友谊能产生巨大力量；这一话题也可能涉及友情双方的变化，以及自己对友情友谊的反思和感悟。

一、构建语料库

(一)词汇短语

1. 单词

appreciate	v. 感激	fascinate	v. (使)着迷；(使)迷住
communicate	v. 交流	favour	n. 好感；喜爱；赞同；恩惠 v. 喜爱；支持；赞成
companion	n. 同伴；伴侣；旅伴	forgive	v. 原谅；宽恕
conflict	v. 冲突	fun	n. 享乐；乐趣 adj. 给人欢乐的；有趣的
emotional	adj. 情绪(上)的；情感(上)的；感情用事的	grateful	adj. 感激的；感谢的
enjoyable	adj. 令人愉快的；有乐趣的	greet	v. 打招呼；问候；迎接
enthusiasm	n. 热情；热忱	introduce	v. 介绍；引进

enthusiastic	adj.（充满）热情的；热心的	misunderstand	v. 误解；误会
fan	n.（运动、电影等的）狂热爱好者；迷	part	v. 分手；告别；（使）分开
farewell	n. 告别	refuse	v. 拒绝

2. 词组

apologise（to sb.）for（doing）sth.	因为（做）某事（向某人）道歉
ask sb. a favour	请某人帮一个忙
be enthusiastic about sth.	对某事充满了热情
be grateful to sb. for sth.	感谢某人
be highly praised for	因……获得高度赞扬
be on good terms（with sb.）	（与某人）关系好
beyond one's expectations	出乎某人意料地
break friendship with	与……断交
do sb. a favour	帮某人一个忙
for company	作伴；陪伴
for fun	为了玩乐
form a friendship	建立友谊
go one's separate ways	断绝往来；分道而行
greet sb. with…	和某人打招呼
have a lot in common	有许多共同之处
have fun	作乐；玩乐
in company with	与……一起
in favour of	赞同；支持
in high spirits	兴高采烈
in low spirits	意志消沉
introduce sb./sth. to	介绍某人/某物
introduce sth. to/into	引起某物
keep company with	和……结交
keep in touch（with）	（与……）保持联系

let sb. down	使失望;辜负
lose heart	灰心
make fun of	取笑;拿……开玩笑
owe sb. sth./owe sth. to sb.	应该给某人某物/欠某人某物
refuse to do sth.	拒绝做某事
say goodbye to	向……告别
see sb. off	为某人送行
shoulder the blame for sth.	对某事承担责任
sing high praise for	高度赞扬
take care	注意;当心;走好;保重
to sb's delight/to the delight of sb.	令某人高兴的是
win sb's favour	赢得某人的好感/欢心

(二)情景句式

①True friendship comes from genuine care and love for each other.

真正的友谊来自于对彼此真正的关心和爱。

②Maybe it won't be so bad to have a new person in my corner of the world after all.

也许在世界上属于我的角落有一个新朋友也是非常好的。

③I have learned a lesson from the experience that a strong relationship starts with two people who are ready to sacrifice anything for each other.

我在这次经历中吸取了教训,一段牢固的关系始于两个准备为彼此牺牲的人。

④Although we are not blood relatives, the tie between us is even stronger than that.

虽然我们不是血亲,但我们之间的关系甚至比那更紧密。

⑤Looking back, I am always grateful for her making up with me.

回顾过去我很感激她站出来与我和好。

⑥The language of friendship is not words but meanings.

友谊的语言不是语言而是意义。

⑦Friendship consists in forgetting what one gives and remembering what one receives.

友谊在于忘记一个人给予了什么,记住一个人接受了什么。

⑧Anybody can sympathize with the sufferings of a friend, but it requires a very fine nature to sympathize with a friend's success.

任何人都能同情朋友的痛苦，但认可朋友的成功需要一个非常好的天性。

二、语篇分析

阅读下面材料，根据其内容和所给段落开头语续写两段，使之构成一篇完整的短文。

Our friendship runs back to our college days when I first met Rishi. We had our own share first impression abouteach other. Mine was—she's a lovely, charming and full of life personality. Hers was—I look like an arrogant personality. I don't blame her for this. Many of my close friends had the same view when they first met me. Blame it on my bitch face and me being a shy person to some extent.

We became really close within a short period of time. Ours was group of four people divided into 2 each during our final year when we both chose advertising as our specialization and the other two journalism. Back then, I was a regular user of BBM messenger and hardly used Whatsapp.

On one specific occasion, we had really bad argument about a failed project. The usual blame game was on. We decided to put it past us and focus on our studies. During this time, she once handed me her phone to show me a picture. While I was going through that, I came across a message from a particular Whats app group that comprises of her and my other two friends. I asked her permission to view the group. She had a blank expression on her face. But she allowed me to go ahead.

I was in shock while going through their messages. Not really positive things were said about me in particular. It shook me. Because these were the people. I considered my friends. I broke down in front of her. Sheapologized. But I felt cheated on. I told her about my decision of not wanting to continue this friendship further. We both missed each other. But neither of us wanted to give the last try.

注意：
1.续写词数应为150左右
2.请按如下格式在答题卡的相应位置作答

Then came our official last trip.

It's 7 years after graduation since we picked up our friendship.

三、文本故事架构

本文属于"人与社会"——"良好的人际关系和社会交往"下的"友情友谊　包容合作"话题。文章记叙了作者"我"和 Rishi 友谊恢复的经历。考生在阅读这类文本时,应把握故事发展的三条线,即时空线、故事情节线和情感发展线。

（一）时空线

时间和空间转换跨度较大:大学校园,旅途中和毕业后 7 年。

（二）故事情节线

本文以人物为线索展开,讲述了作者和 Rishi 在大学成了好朋友,一次作者无意中看到了 Rishi 和另外两个朋友组成的群消息,群里对作者的评价并不是很正面,这让作者很受伤,不想再和 Rishi 继续当朋友了。最后在一次旅行中作者和 Rishi 化解了矛盾,友谊一直持续到了现在。

（三）情感发展线

大学一段时间好朋友→作业项目失败起争端→浏览负面讯息友情破裂→最后一次旅行→Rishi 主动拥抱了作者→作者和 Rishi 和好→Rishi 和作者的友谊持续至今。

四、关键信息梳理

（一）人物

语篇出现了的人物是"我"和 Rishi。

文本中的关键词有:"我"是本文主人公,Rishi 是关键人物。friendship,college,shock,friends,view 等。这些词汇在续写故事情节的形成和发展过程中,起着非常重要的作用,抓住了这些关键词就抓住了续写的思路。

（二）提示句分析

由第一段首句内容"Then came our official last trip"可知,接下来是旅行,是"我们"正式的最后一次旅行。第一段可描写作者和 Rishi 在这次旅行中的经历和体会。

由第二段首句内容"It's 7 years after graduation since we picked up our friendship"可知,从"我们"开始"我们"的友谊到现在已经快 7 年了。第二段

可描写和 Rishi 的友谊带给作者的感悟。

五、写作思路构建

我们开始了正式的最后一次旅行,这次旅行使我们重新认识自我。我和 Rishi 在这次旅行中的经历、体会和感悟良多。从我们开始我们的友谊到现在已经快 7 年了,7 年来,我们相互支持,互相牵挂,彼此珍惜这份友谊。

(一)习作欣赏

Then came our official last trip. I hanged out with my other friends while she with the other two girls. I wasn't enjoying this trip at all, which she could make out. When she saw me approaching the common washroom, she followed me in. I didn't know how to react. She gave me a tight hug and broke down. My tears were also out of control. We knew we both wanted to be in each other's company. We promised to grow mature and let it not affect our friendship.

It's 7 years after graduation since we picked up our friendship. She's one of the few people I really count on in my life. She's been with me through all my struggles, helping me constantly to grow into a better individual. So have I. The only learning from our relationship is—if someone is meant to be in your life, they will ensure they stay around some way or the other. Willingness to keep a relationship should come from both the sides.

(二)习作评价

续写部分思路清晰,与文本的融洽度高,定语从句、状语从句等优秀句子结构多,hanged out、approaching、a tight hug、broke down、out of control 等词汇丰富。

第六节　志愿服务　公益事业

"志愿服务　公益事业"是"人与社会"—"社会服务与人际沟通"主题语境下的重要话题,是新高考读后续写命题的重要语境。这种语境下,学生的情感态度得以体现,服务社会,服务别人的意识不断增强。

一、构建语料库

(一)词汇短语

1. 单词

achieve	v.（凭借努力）达到	manage	v. 设法做成；努力完成
achievement	n. 完成；功绩；成就	reward	n. 回报；报酬；v. 报答；奖赏
aid	n. 援助；救助；v. 帮助	voluntary	adj. 志愿的；自愿的
ambition	n. 野心；雄心；抱负	volunteer	v. 自愿（做某事）；n. 志愿者
ambitious	adj. 有抱负的；野心勃勃的	welcome	v. 欢迎；迎接 adj. 受欢迎的；令人愉快的
determined	adj. 决意的；坚决的；坚定的	will	n. 意志；决心
engaged	adj. 被占用的；忙于；从事于	worthwhile	adj. 值得花时间/精力的
experience	n. 经历；经验；v. 经历；体验（到）		

2. 词组

(be) determined to do sth.	决意去做某事
a sense of achievement	成就感
achieve success	取得成功
apply/devote one's energies into/to a job	致力于一项工作
be absorbed in	专注于……
be aware of	意识到；知道
be rewarded (with sth.)	得到回报
be thankful for	感激……
catch up with	追上；赶上
come/go to sb's aid	来帮助某人
do sb. a favour	帮某人一个忙
experience failure/success	经历失败/成功
in return (for sth.)	作为（……的）交换（回报）
keep up/lose courage	鼓足/失去勇气

make every effort to	尽一切努力
make progress	取得进步
make up one's mind	作出决定;下定决心
owe…to	把……归功于
pay off	取得成功;得到好结果
personal experience	个人经历
put effort into	把精力放在……
spare no effort to do sth.	不遗余力做某事
stick to	坚持;遵守
take pains to do sth.	努力/下苦功做某事
turn out	原来(是);证明(是);结果(是)
volunteer to do sth.	自愿做某事
with an intention of	目的是

(二)情景句式

①Selfless love, unlimited hope. 无私的爱心,无限的希望。

②I participate in the volunteer service, and I am happy!
志愿服务,我参与,我快乐!

③Learn moral models and be good people around you.
学道德模范,做身边好人。

④The same love to you, pass on. Don't stop all the way!
同样的爱心送给你,传递下去。一路别停!

⑤Reach out your warm hand and open the door of love.
伸出温暖手,打开爱心门。

⑥Love is born in the heart, and the heart takes love as its soul.
爱自心中生,心以爱作魂。

⑦If our hearts are full of love, then our hearts are full of flowers.
如果我们心中充满爱,那么,我们的心里就开满鲜花。

⑧Often we can't do great things, but we can do little things with great love.
我们常常无法做伟大的事,但我们可以用伟大的爱去做些小事。

⑨Love is the best stage for volunteers, and dedication is the most beautiful language for volunteers.
爱心是志愿者最好的舞台,奉献是志愿者最美的语言。

⑩Service, volunteer, it's enough to have such an experience in my life.

服务,志愿者,在我的人生中有这样一段经历就足够了。

二、语篇分析

阅读下面材料,根据其内容和所给段落开头语续写两段,使之构成一篇完整的短文。

One morning on our way to school, there was an elderly woman dressed in a yellow vest (马甲) carrying a garbage bag and one of those rubbish claws(垃圾爪). "What's that lady doing?" I asked mum.

"Vest Lady. She just picks up rubbish around here for fun," mum said.

"Why would someone think picking up rubbish looking like a construction workeris fun?" I puzzled.

For several years I'd witness this mysterious Vest Lady — rain or shine — on my way to school. I had thought she was crazy for picking up rubbish. Gradually I smiled and waved at her each time I saw her.

Later, I moved tohigh school. The time I saw rubbish here and there I felt really annoyed. Then I'd think, "Why isn't anyone picking up this rubbish? People are so inconsiderate!" However, shortly after, I realized picking up the rubbish was not someone else's problem.

Now Icould't walk past litter without feeling guilty. I volunteered to clean up rubbish around our school. As strange as it might sound, picking up litter was kind of a thrill for me! In fact, I was so determined that for my 17th birthday I bought myself a rubbish claw, reusable gloves and a reflective safety yellow vest with my own name on it.

During my firstattempt in my stylish equipment, I met with unfriendly looks from others as if I were a criminal doing community service. One day, I had an e-piphany(顿悟): "I'm acting just like Vest Lady!"

But there was too much rubbish around, cigarette ends littered about, cans rolling on the street, pieces of paper hidden in the grass and plastic…. I alone was too weak! How would I organize more volunteers in rubbish removal? A smart idea came to my mind.

注意:

1. 续写词数应为150左右

2. 请按如下格式在答题卡的相应位置作答

> Soon I created my website：go. picking up. com.
>
> More and more people put on theVest with their names.

三、文本故事架构

本文属于"人与社会"主题语境的"志愿服务"话题。文章记叙了"我"受马甲太太影响,志愿清扫垃圾的故事。考生在阅读这类文本时,应把握故事发展的三条线,即时空线、故事情节线和情感发展线。

（一）时空线

小时候到中学,在学校周围。

（二）故事情节线

小时候上学路上,总发现一位年长的老太太穿着马甲,手里拎着塑料袋,拿着捡垃圾的工具。我不解地问妈妈。妈妈回答是在捡垃圾。多年来,无论下雨还是阳光的日子,我一直见证着这位神秘的马甲女士。

之后,我上了中学,我看到到处都是垃圾,我很生气。于是我会问为什么没有人来这儿捡垃圾。然而,一段时间之后,我意识到了捡垃圾不是别人的问题。我要行动起来,志愿清理学校周围的垃圾。17岁生日的当天,我给自己买了捡垃圾的工具,穿上了印有我名字的马甲。第一次穿上马甲,带着工具捡垃圾,会有不少异样的眼光瞅着我,我就像那一位马甲女士。但是周围的垃圾实在太多了。我个人的力量太渺小！我怎么能够号召更多的志愿者跟我一块儿捡垃圾呢？这时候我有了一个好的主意。

（三）情感发展线

小时候上学路上,发现 Vest Lady 捡垃圾（迷惑不解）→我上了中学,我看到到处都是垃圾（生气）→一段时间之后,意识到了捡垃圾是自己的行动（主动）→垃圾实在太多了,个人的力量渺小（共同努力）。

四、关键信息梳理

（一）人物

语篇出现了3个人物："我",mother,Vest Lady。

（二）提示句分析

根据第一段提示句"Soon I created my website go. picking up. com."我们可以推断出,"我"建立了自己的网站并宣传了自己的活动目的就是号召更多的志愿者参与捡垃圾。

根据第二段提示句"More and more people put on the Vest with their names"我们可以推断出,越来越多的志愿者加入了"我们"的行列。众人拾柴火焰高,在"我们"的共同努力下,"我们"的环境变得越来越好。

五、写作思路构建

我建立了自己的网站,在网站的首页上我表明了我的活动目的是捡垃圾,我们急切招收志愿者加入我们的行动!网站上有简便的报名的方式:通过电话或者是邮件。还有我们清理垃圾前后对比的照片。一些动人的故事也出现在我的网站中。

于是没过几天,我非常激动地发现,越来越多的志愿者加入了我们的行列。越来越多的人穿上了带着自己名字的马甲。这些志愿者在我们学校周围捡垃圾,马甲成了一道靓丽的风景线。众人拾柴火焰高,在我们的共同努力下,我们的环境变得越来越好。使我高兴的是,人们的环保意识也大大增强。

（一）习作欣赏

Soon I created my websitego. picking up. com. On the Home page,I set the purpose of my creation — Pick up rubbish and live in a cleaner world. We eagerly need more volunteers to join in our act! There is easy access to signing up through the internet or by telephone. Posted pictures of rubbish around clearly show how urgent it was to remove the wastes. Remarkable stories about volunteers are also shared on my website. Then with a few days,I was excited to find ever growing volunteers joined us. Even some local companies wanted to offer financial help to our clear up project.

More and more people put on the Vest with their own names. Volunteers of picking up rubbish could be seen around in our spare time. The yellow vests made a beautiful sight in the park or on the street. Together,individuals really made a difference! With our join efforts,the environment became better and better. What delighted me most was that people's awareness of environmental protection is increasingly intense. The rubbish removal campaign was a big success. Thanks to Vest lady,she not only rooted the sense of environmental protection in my mind, but also was a constant reminder and inspiration.

（二）习作评价

续写部分较多使用了优秀句式,语言非常丰富,特别是"Together, individuals really made a difference!"起到了点睛之笔。最后一句："Thanks to

Vest lady, she not only rooted the sense of environmental protection in my mind, but also was a constant reminder and inspiration"呼应了文章开头。

第七节　历险施救　安全常识

　　"人与自然"—"灾害防范"主题语境下"自然灾害与防范、安全常识与自我保护"的话题,是读后续写命题的重要话题,该语境会涉及自救、他救、互救。这些施救的内容包括:危险之际,不慌不乱,利用急救知识,急中生智,化险为夷等。该话题的语言画面感很强,常使用动词、形容词、副词等。

一、构建语料库

(一)词汇短语

1.单词

adventure	n.冒险(经历);奇遇	explore	v.探测;探索;探究
ambulance	n.救护车	fantastic	adj.极好的
attack	v.攻击;袭击	hopeless	adj.无助的
camping	n.露营;野营	impressive	adj.给人深刻印象的;令人钦佩的
circumstance	n.情况;情形	panic	v.惊慌
collision	n.碰撞;冲突	recover	v.复原
crash	v.撞毁	resort	n.度假胜地
dramatically	adv.突然地;急剧地	route	n.路线;路程;航线
emergency	n.紧急情况	scene	n.景色;景象;事发地点;现场
equipment	n.装备;设备	shelter	n.居所;避难所;掩蔽;庇护 v.庇护;为……提供避难所

2.词组

a beautiful scene in nature	自然美景
a power cut/failure	停电
be/get caught in	陷入;被困住
be/get stuck in	卡住;陷入

broaden one's mind	开阔眼界
check in	登记;报到
check out	结账离开;核实
cut off	切掉;切断;使隔绝
fall down	跌倒;倒塌
fall into/get out of a trap	落入/摆脱圈套
feel one's way	摸索而行
follow sb's tracks	跟踪某人
in need	在困难中;在困境中
keep track of	与……保持联系;了解……的动态
lose track of	失去……线索;与……失去联系
miss a flight	赶上飞机/误机
perform the first aid during the emergency	在紧急情况下实施了急救
return ticket	往返票
round trip	往返旅行
search for	搜寻
set out	出发;打算;阐述
shelter...from sb./sth.	保护……免受……
take it easy	不紧张;从容;不急
take measures to do sth.	采取措施做某事
take shelter from the rain	避雨
take/follow a route	走某条路线
to make matters worse	使情况更糟的是
turn to	转向;求助于
under the shelter of	在……下躲着
wide awake	毫无睡意
work out	解决;把……弄清楚
work together	共同工作
worry about	担心;忧虑

(二)情景句式

①Lay her on their back and check for breathing. 让她平躺,检查呼吸状况。

②She was lying unconscious on the ground, leaving her friends in a panic. 她躺在地上,没有了意识,这让朋友们惊慌失措。

③Nervous and anxious, he struggled to calm herself down and carried out first aid to Simmons.

尽管紧张而焦虑,他努力让自己镇静下来,对 Simmons 进行了急救。

④After what seemed to be half an hour, Simmons regained her consciousness.

似乎过了半小时,Simmons 恢复了知觉。

⑤A thick burning smell filled the air. 空气里弥漫着浓厚灼热的味道。

⑥Watching the shore in the distance, I felt powerless as if we were broken tiny boats at the mercy of strong waves.

看着远处的海岸,我感到无能为力,就好像我们是被强浪摧毁的小船一样。

⑦Exhausted and cold, the thought that we might die here flashed across my mind.

筋疲力尽,寒冷,我有了我们可能死在这里的想法。

⑧We exchanged our firm look, then moved on at an incredible speed.
相互坚定地看看对方,以难以置信的速度继续前行。

⑨What's worse, he didn't have any food or water with him, Not to mention his cell phone and other necessities.

更糟糕的是,他没有带水和食品,更不要说他的手机和其他日用品了。

⑩Ultimately, we were back, safe and sound 最终我们安然无恙地回来了。

⑪Seeing Simmons wake up from passing out, Norwood breathed a sigh of relief.

看到 Simmons 从昏倒中醒来,Norwood 松了一口气。

⑫Simmons showed her gratitude to Norwood, saying "It was you who came to my aid and saved my life. "

Simmons 对 Norwood 表示了感谢,她说:"是你来帮助我,救了我一命。"

⑬The story shows that a good knowledge of first aid can make a real difference.

这个故事表明,良好的急救知识真的可以起作用。

⑭We have learnt from the incident that life is valuable and the skill of saving is more valuable.

我们从这件事中学到生命非常有价值,拯救的技能更有价值。

二、语篇分析

2020 年 7 月浙江高考题

阅读下面材料,根据其内容和所给段落开头语续写两段,使之构成一篇完整的短文。

One fall, my wife Elli and I had a single goal: to photograph polar bears. We were staying at a research camp outside "the polar bear capital of the world" – the town of Churchill in Manitoba, Canada.

Taking pictures of polar bears is amazing but also dangerous. Polar bears like all wild animals—should be photographed from a safe distance. When I'm face to face with a polar bear, I like it to be through a camera with a telephoto lens. But sometimes, that is easier said than done. This was one of those times.

As Elli and I cooked dinner, a young male polar bear who was playing in a nearby lake sniffed, and smelled our garlic bread.

The hungry bear followed his nose to our camp, which was surrounded by a high wire fence. Hepulled and bit the wire. He stood on his back legs and pushed at the wooden fence posts.

Terrified, Eli and I tried all the bear defense actions we knew. We yelled at the bear, hit pots hard, and fired blank shotgun shells into the air. Sometimes loud noises like these will scare bears off. Not this polar bear though—he just kept trying to tear down the fence with his massive paws (爪子).

I radioed the camp manager for help. He told me a helicopter was on its way, but it would be 30 minutes before it arrived. Making the best of this close encounter (相遇), I took some pictures of the bear.

Elli and I feared the fence wouldn't last through 30 more minutes of the bear's punishment. The camp manager suggested I use pepper spray. The spray burns the bears' eyes, but doesn't hurt them. So I approached our uninvited guest slowly and, through the fence, sprayed him in the face. With an angry roar (吼叫), the bear ran to the lake to wash his eyes.

注意:

1. 续写词数应为 150 左右

2.请按如下格式在答题卡的相应位置作答

> A few minutes later, the bear headed back to our camp.
> At that very moment, the helicopter arrived.

三、文本故事架构

本文属于"人与自然"—"人与动物"主题语境下的"安全常识与自我保护"话题。主要讲了"我"与妻子 Elli 到一个研究营地拍摄北极熊照片,准备晚饭时,一只北极熊意欲闯入,"我们"和北极熊对峙较量的过程。文本体现了作者热爱自然,爱护动物的情怀。考生在阅读这类文本时,应把握故事发展的三条线,即时空线、故事情节线和情感发展线。

(一)时空线

在一个秋天,我们到研究营地去拍摄北极熊照片,在做晚饭的时候发生的事情。

One fall in a research camp→As...cooked dinner, a hungry bear followed to our camp→I radioed the camp manager for help→A few minutes later→At that very moment, the helicopter arrived。

(二)故事情节线

我们正在做晚饭,一只雄性的北极熊闻到了做饭的味道,来到了我们的驻地,隔着栅栏和铁丝网,北极熊发起了攻击。我和妻子尝试做出各种应对方法,未果;无计可施,便向营地经理求助。最快的直升机也需要 30 分钟到达。我按照营地经理给出的自救方案:向北极熊撒胡椒粉,暂时驱赶走了北极熊。几分钟后,北极熊再次来袭,且更加恼火。一场人与北极熊之间的对峙较量即将展开。

(三)情感发展线

去拍摄北极熊的照片(令人惊喜,非常危险)→雄性北极熊出现,破坏围栏(惊恐)→尝试制造各种防御措施,未果(恐惧)→向营地经理求助,北极熊越来越咆哮(绝望)→喷洒辣椒水,北极熊后退(欣慰)→北极熊卷土重来(紧张恐惧)→直升机到达(欣慰)。

四、关键信息梳理

(一)人物

语篇出现了 4 个人、物:"我"、妻子 Elli、camp manager 以及北极熊。其中"我"、妻子和北极熊是关键人物,应贯穿全文。

文本中的关键词有:Elli,photograph,camera,pictures,safe,fence 和 ran 等。根据故事的发展和提示句,我们推断出 Elli 和作者密不可分,photograph,pictures,camera,fence 是本文的非常关键的要素,作者和妻子安全脱险,因此 safe 要素不可缺少,ran 是重要的动词。

(二)提示句分析

根据第一段提示句"A few minutes later,the bear headed back to our camp"我们可以推断出,北极熊的这次攻击更猛烈,因此本段主要描写北极熊攻击的动作和猛烈的程度,以此映衬出作者和妻子应对北极熊袭击的心理活动和智慧。

根据第二段提示句"At that very moment,the helicopter arrived"我们可以推断出,直升机的到来给"我"和妻子带来了希望。在十分危机时刻出现了积极变化,因此本段主要写夫妇获救的曲折过程,以及获救后的心理活动。

五、写作思路构建

(一)思路一

几分钟之后,这只北极熊又回到我们的营地。这一次比以往凶得多,北极熊咆哮着,激烈地撕咬着篱笆,最终把篱笆咬破了一个口子,我和妻子绝望地瘫在地上。在这十分危险的时刻,我们听到了前来救援的直升机! 在救护人员的帮助下,我和妻子匆匆忙忙地走上了飞机。看到那只饥饿的北极熊失望地望着我们,我拿起相机又拍了一张照片。可是看着相片中饥饿的北极熊,我又心生怜悯。

1. 习作欣赏

A few minutes later,the bear came back. With two bloodshot eyes,he let out a deafening roar and violently charged at the fence with his full strength. I really had my heart in my mouth. We have no alternative but to anxiously wait for the helicopter. With cracking noises,the bear rushed in,approaching us rapidly. We tried pepper spray again,but in vain. With the bear chasing behind,"Elli,come on,"I yelled,attracting the bear to an opposite direction,but unfortunately,I was trapped to a narrow corner,where I could almost hear the gasps of it.

At the very moment,the helicopter arrived. No sooner had we seen the helicopter in the sky when we felt relieved to know we would be saved. Several gunshots echoed to scare it off. The bear lifted his face and stared at the giant figure of the helicopter. Slowly,he draw back. Relieved yet exhausted,I climbed into the helicopter safe, hugging tightly with Elli. It was such a breathtaking experience, but as I developed the film later, all just became worthwhile.

2. 习作评价

三个连续动词 let out, charged at, shoved 的使用,勾画出了北极熊的疯狂形象。"We have no alternative but to anxiously wait for the helicopter" 优秀句式的运用将"我"和妻子绝望的绝望之情溢于言表。危急时刻,绝处逢生,直升机的到来带来了希望。接下来的动作描写非常细致,生动刻画了"深陷危机到平安救出"的过程。特别指出的是,续写部分使用了非常多的优秀句式和词汇,语言丰富多彩。

(二)思路二

几分钟之后,这只北极熊又回到我们的营地。这一次比以往凶的多,北极熊咆哮着,激烈地撕咬着篱笆,我和妻子恐惧到了极点,我握着枪随时准备应对不测! 但妻子提醒我不要伤害北极熊。在这十分危险的时刻,前来救援的直升机到了! 我和妻子匆匆忙忙地走上了飞机。那只饥饿的北极熊好奇地望着我们,没有了刚才的凶狠,似乎是为我们送行!

1. 习作欣赏

A few minutes later, the bear came back. As the spray had been used up, we were confined into a desperate stage. With little weapon to defend ourselves in this temporary camp, Eilli and I were nearly dead with fright, when the angry bear smashed the fence once and once again. Ultimately, he made it. To our surprise, the bear ran straight towards the leftovers of our dinner, leaving us precious time to run to a safer shelter in the camp.

At the very moment, the helicopter arrived. With a loud bang, the beast fell down. We quickly boarded the helicopter and finally breathed a sigh of relief. Had it not been for the staff's timely shot, we might not have survived the bear's massive paws. It took time to calm ourselves down and it brought us great relief to know that the bear hadn't been killed. It was only a mild medicine injected to make it fall asleep. Looking at the pictures we took, we found the bear were emotional like us human. It was really an unforgettable experience.

2. 习作评价

面对北极熊的疯狂袭击,续写第一段生动刻画了危急时刻的心理活动。a desperate stage, nearly dead with fright, to our surprise 等词汇使用也很地道。第二段写出了获救的过程和获救后的喜悦。with a loud bang, breathed a sigh of relief 用词非常生动,形象。

第八节 人与动物 和谐共处

　　"人与自然"—"自然生态"主题语境中"人与动物"和谐共处是高考常考的话题之一。野生动植物在现代社会面临着巨大的威胁。人类活动的影响、气候的变化使野生动植物的数量急剧减少,保护野生动植物是我们每个人的责任和义务。读后续写中所涉及的人与动物是和谐有机的整体,是相互依存的统一体,保护野生动物,体现人与动物和谐统一是考试的方向。

一、构建语料库

(一)词汇短语

1. 单词

ant	n.蚂蚁	habitat	n.(动物)栖息地
bark	v.狗叫;狗吠	hatch	v.孵出;孵(卵)
bear	n.熊	herd	n.兽群;牧群
bird	n.鸟	hiss	v.嘶嘶声
bite	v. & n.咬	howl	v.(狗、狼等)嚎叫;n.嚎叫
breed	v.繁殖;生育;饲养	insect	n.昆虫;虫
bull	n.公牛	lamb	n.羔羊,小羊
bush	n.矮灌木;灌木丛	leaf	n.叶子
butterfly	n.蝴蝶	lion	n.狮子
calf	n.小牛	lion	n.狮子
camel	n.骆驼	mammal	n.哺乳动物
cat	n.猫	mouse	n.老鼠
cattle	n.牲畜;牛	panda	n.熊猫
challenge	n.挑战	paw	n.(猫、狗、熊等动物的)爪
consequence	n.后果	rabbit	n.兔子
creature	n.生物	roar	v.咆哮
creature	n.生物;动物	scared	adj.对……感到惊慌的;吓坏了的
disappearance	n.消失	scream	v.尖叫着说;(风)呼啸 n.尖叫声

elephant	n.大象	species	n.物种
environment	n.环境	survival	n.幸存;存活……
extinction	n.灭绝	tame	adj.驯服的
fly	n.苍蝇	tiger	n.老虎
fox	n.狐狸	turkey	n.火鸡
frog	n.青蛙	wag	v.摇尾巴
giraffe	n.长颈鹿	whale	n.鲸
goat	n.山羊	wild	adj.野生的
goose	n.鹅	wolf	n.狼

2. 词组

(be) scared of (doing) sth.	害怕(做)某事
attach treat importance to	十分重视……
in harmony with nature	与自然和谐相处
scream in/with fear	吓得尖叫
take effective measures	采取有效措施
wildlife reserve	野生动物保护区

(二)情景句式

①A canary was singing in a cage. 金丝雀在笼子里唱歌。

②The rabbit was caught in a trap. 兔子被捕捉器夹住了。

③The kitten was black, with white paws. 小猫是黑色的,猫爪是白色的。

④The bird flew away as I came near. 当我走近时,鸟儿飞走了。

⑤The deer never became tame;they ran away if you went near them.
鹿从来没有被驯服,当你走近时,它们会逃跑。

⑥The sun bird's mouth was very strange, long and sharp, slightly curved.
太阳鸟的嘴巴生得十分奇特,又尖又长,略微有点弯曲。

⑦Monkeys often stay in trees and jump between them. They are so lively and favorable.
猴子常常待在树上,在树木之间跳来跳去,非常活泼,讨人喜欢。

⑧The little cat's head is round, with a pair of pointed ears, and the big green eyes look like two green lights.

小花猫的脑袋圆圆的,顶着一对尖尖的小耳朵,那大大的绿眼睛瞪得像两盏小绿灯。

⑨The little black dog,black and shiny,is as smooth as black satin,whose tail is always swinging.

那条小黑狗,一身乌黑发亮的皮毛,就像黑缎子一般油亮光滑;那条小尾巴,总是悠闲不停地摇摆着。

⑩Only when much attention has been paid to wildlife protection,can we live in harmony with nature.

只有充分重视野生生物的保护,我们才能与自然和谐相处。

二、语篇分析

2020 年 1 月浙江高考卷

阅读下面材料,根据其内容和所给段落开头语续写两段,使之构成一篇完整的短文。

"I'm going to miss you so much,Poppy," said the tall, thin teenager. He bent down to hug his old friend goodbye. He stood up, hugged his parents, and smiled, trying not to let his emotions(情绪) get the better of him.

His parents were not quite able to keep theirs under control. They had driven their son several hours out of town to the university where he would soon be living and studying. It was time to say goodbye for now at least. The family hugged and smiled through misty eyes and then laughed.

The boy lifted the last bag onto his shoulder, and flashed a bright smile. "I guess this is it," he said. "I'll see you back home in a month, okay?" His parents nodded, and they watched as he walked out of sight into the crowds of hundreds of students and parents. The boy's mother turned to the dog, "Okay, Poppy, time to go back home."

The house seemed quiet as a tomb without the boy living there. All that week, Poppy didn't seem interested in her dinner, her favorite toy, or even in her daily walk. Her owners were sad too, but they knew their son would be back to visit. Poppy didn't.

They offered the dog some of her favorite peanut butter treats. They even let her sit on the sofa, but the old girl just wasn't her usual cheerful self. Her owners started to get worried. "What should we do to cheer Poppy up?" asked Dad. "We are tried everything."

"I have an idea, but it might be a little crazy," smiled Mom. "Without anybody left in the house but us, this place could use a bit of fun. Let's get a little dog for Poppy.

It didn't take long before they walked through the front door carrying a big box. Poppy welcomed them home as usual but when she saw the box, she stopped. She put her nose on it. Her tail began wagging(摆动) ever so slowly, then faster as she caught the smell.

注意:

1. 续写词数应为 150 左右

2. 请按如下格式在答题卡的相应位置作答

> Dad opened the box and a sweet little dog appeared.
>
> A few weeks later, the boy arrived home from university.

三、文本故事架构

本文属于"人与自然"—"自然生态"主题语境下的"人与动物"话题。主要讲了男孩离家上大学,家中狗狗郁郁寡欢,男孩的父母为了让狗狗高兴起来,又找了一只小狗做伴。故事表达了狗狗对小主人的忠诚和依恋,同时又体现出父母对男孩离家后的不舍。本文以小狗为线索,表达了父母与子女浓浓的亲情,体现了人与动物不可分割的感情。考生在阅读这类文本时,应把握故事发展的三条线,即时空线、故事情节线和情感发展线。

(一)时空线

故事发生在家中。

男孩吻别 Poppy 和家人去求学,父母带着宠物狗送行→男孩离家,家里冷清,Poppy 闷闷不乐→女主人给 Poppy 找个伴,Poppy 的生活步入正轨→男孩回家。

(二)故事情节线

男孩吻别 Poppy 和家人,即将离家奔赴大学所在城市,父母带着宠物狗 Poppy 去送他。男孩与父母依依惜别,含泪(smile with misty eyes)拥抱。男孩离开后,家里冷清的环境让 Poppy 闷闷不乐。女主人心生一计,想要给 Poppy 找个伴。男孩的父母回家时 Poppy 照常到门口迎接,此时她突然闻到了小狗的味道……

(三)情感发展线

故事主人公情感的变化经历了以下过程:

男孩吻别 Poppy 和家人去求学,父母带着宠物狗送行(依依惜别)→男孩离家,家里冷清,Poppy 闷闷不乐(孤独、思念)→主人给 Poppy 找个伴(快乐)→男孩回家团聚(激动)。

四、关键信息梳理

(一)人物

语篇出现的角色是小男孩,狗狗 Poppy 和父母,但最关键的是小男孩和狗狗。

可以选出的关键词是 Poppy,parents,boy,dog,hugged,cheerful,等。这些是文本中的关键人物,是贯穿故事的重要线索。hugged 是文本的重要动作词汇,cheerful 体现主人公和狗狗相逢愉悦情感的形容词。

(二)提示句分析

根据第一段提示句"Dad opened the box and a sweet little dog appeared"我们可以推断出,新伙伴的到来,Poppy 的变化。续写的内容:狗狗对新伙伴的欢迎,兴奋。再写没有小主人的日子情感有了寄托,情绪终于稳定下来。

根据第二段提示句"A few weeks later, the boy arrived home from university"我们可以推断出,几周之后,男孩从大学回家。续写的内容:父母与子女浓浓的亲情,小主人与狗狗的不可分割的感情,奠定了男孩回家的情感和心理、动作。而狗狗与小主人重逢的喜悦也是浓墨重彩的一笔。

五、写作思路构建

思路一:Poppy 如何迎接男孩回家(leans against his leg/both paws on his body/licking/barking with excitement)

思路二:小狗第一次见到男孩的反应(hide in a box,observe curiously);在 Poppy 的鼓励下接受男孩,一家人团聚。

(一)习作欣赏

Dad opened the box and a sweet little dog appeared. Poppy's tail wagged even faster. Meanwhile, a warm glow of satisfaction appeared on Poppy's face. Gradually, Poppy calmed down and watched the little dog with tenderness, as if she were a dedicated mother. The little dog returned Poppy's love with affection of his own, walking slowly and leaning on her. The parents were relieved to feel the sweetness of the dogs mixed with their longing for their sons' return.

A few weeks later, the boy arrived home from university. He dashed into the house like an arrow and shouted in a cheerful voice: "Mom, Dad, Poppy!"

Naturally, he threw himself into his parents' arms and hugged them tightly. With cheerful barks, Poppy twisted her body dramatically, bouncing up to the height of the boy's knees, constantly licking his hand. Strange it might seem, she suddenly turned around and ran away. The boy curiously followed and saw the sweet little dog curled in the corner. As a precious gift, the sweet warmed the cockles of their heart.

(二)习作评价

新狗狗的到来,让 Poppy 兴奋不已,表达兴奋情感词汇的使用,使狗狗的活泼可爱的形象跃然纸上。小主人放学回家,使用了非常形象的动词,人物的刻画也细致入微,回家团聚的情景非常温馨。

附录 1　参考文献

[1]中华人民共和国教育部.普通高中英语课程标准(2017 年版 2020 年修订)[M].北京:人民教育出版社,2020.

[2]王蔷,胡亚林,陈则航.基于学生核心素养的英语学科能力研究[M].北京:北京师范大学出版社,2018.

[3]李运兴.语篇翻译引论[M].北京:中国对外翻译出版公司,2001.

[4]胡壮麟,语篇的衔接与连贯[M].上海:上海外语教育出版社,1994.

[5]黄国文.语篇分析概要[M].长沙:湖南教育出版社,1988.

[6]王小丽.拉波夫的叙事分析模式在语篇分析教学中的应用研究:以语篇《Face to Face with Guns》为例[J].兵团教育学院学报,2013(6):56-58,73.

[7]王初明.互动协同与外语教学[J].外语教学与研究(北京外国语大学学报),2010,42(4):297-299.

[8]王文伟.基于互动协同效应的读后续写契合点探究教学实践[J].英语学习(教师版),2019(6):50-56.

[9]王敏,王初明.读后续写的协同效应[J].现代外语,2014,37(4):501-512.

[10]姜琳,陈锦.读后续写对英语写作语言准确性、复杂性和流利性发展的影响[J].现代外语,2015,38(3):366-375,438.

[11]龚亚夫,罗少茜.课程理论、社会建构主义理论与任务型语言教学[J].课程·教材·教法,2003,23(1):49-53.

附录 2   读后续写"三步五环节"教学法

一、提出的问题

读后续写教学应遵循怎样的程序和步骤才更有效?

二、问题提出的背景

英语写作是英语学习的重要内容,《普通高中英语课程标准》对写作教学规定了具体目标。基于课程的总目标,普通高中英语课程的具体目标是培养和发展学生在接受高中英语教育后应具备的语言能力、文化意识、思维品质、学习能力等学科核心素养。普通高中英语学科核心素养各要素的发展以三个水平划分。通过本课程的学习,学生应能达到本学段英语课程标准所设定的四项学科核心素养的发展目标。其中,语言能力目标:具有一定的语言意识和英语语感,在常见的具体语境中整合性地运用已有语言知识,理解口头和书面语篇所表达的意义,识别其恰当表意所采用的手段,有效地使用口语和书面语表达意义和进行人际交流。

新一轮课程改革也对写作教学提出了更高的要求,但读后续写教学一直是困扰师生的一大难题。在实际英语教学中,教师轻视写作教学的现象普遍存在,也有的教师不注意规律和方法,写作教学的随意性强,这加大了写作的难度,使学生产生了畏难情绪,也让学生失去了写作的兴趣。多年来,从事英语教学的教师和研究人员也一直在探索一种符合英语学习规律,废时少、见效快的英语写作教学新路子,不少人付出了艰辛的努力。本项目就是在这种背景下提出的提高英语写作教学的新途径。

三、解决问题的内容与实施

以上问题是由于教师不注意探求写作规律和方法所引发的。实际上,英语写作有很强的规律性,英语词汇的使用、短语的搭配、句式的选择和篇章的构思都应循序渐进,不可拔苗助长。针对以上情况,根据学生的学习特点,借助任务型英语写作教学和小组合作探究教学的做法,遵循英语学习循序渐进的学习规律和语言习得理论,本项目设计了解决高中英语写作问题的"三步五环节"教学法。下面将具体介绍。

"三步"指的是要训练学生写作的三个阶段:句子结构正确阶段、语言流畅得体阶段、篇章逻辑严密阶段。"三步"是根据班级学生的写作基础确立的,时间可长可短,总过程为一年。

"句子结构正确"阶段就是在一定时期内,训练学生写出语法正确,结构完整的句子,尤其是动词的时态和语态以及搭配等。在这一阶段,老师强化对学生的五种基本句型的训练:①主语+谓语;②主语+谓语+宾语;③主语+谓语+间接宾语;④主语+谓语+间接宾语+直接宾语;⑤主语+谓语+宾语+补足语。这一阶段除了注意学生习作中的时态和语态以及搭配外,还要训练学生避免介词、名词、形容词、副词等词性错误以及主谓一致、非谓语动词、句式等错误。

"语言流畅得体"阶段就是在一定时期内,训练学生写出语言流畅得体,符合英语表达的句式,避免汉语式的句子和生搬硬套背诵的句式,不要为用高级词汇、高级句型而用,意义的表达更为重要,自然的表达更地道。而培养跨文化交际能力是英语教学的终极目标,新课程标准强调语言的得体性是适应时代发展的需要。同时,在整篇文章中,避免只使用单一句型,要灵活运用各种语法结构,做到句式丰富多彩,长短句相间,简单句与复合句相协调,使文章有声有色,不落俗套。

"篇章逻辑严密"阶段是在一定时期内,训练学生写出上下文连贯、逻辑严谨的篇章。怎样的文章算得上是好文章呢?就百词的小文章来说,语篇的衔接连贯与逻辑严密是十分重要的标准,整篇文章应有效地使用语句间的连接成分,使全文结构紧凑;衔接和连贯是构成语篇的最基本条件。语篇衔接主要体现在四个方面:照应,省略和替代,词汇衔接还有逻辑关系语。

"五环节"指的是每节(45分钟)写作课遵循的五个步骤:背景展示→限时写作→报告任务→反馈评价→完善感悟。

背景展示(10分钟):就是把写作话题交给学生,头脑风暴,激活重点词汇、句型等,为下一步篇章写作做准备。

限时写作(20分钟):写作过程给学生限定时间,让学生有时间观念。教师在教室内观察,并随时提供帮助。

报告任务(8分钟):学习小组内学生交换作文,相互评阅,找出优点和不足,相互学习,合作探究。学生上台投影展示同伴作品,汇报阅读同伴作品后的心得。教师在一旁聆听并作适当评价,就习作中所出现的典型问题师生共同探讨。

反馈评价(5分钟):教师投影展示学生上交的二次写作的作品,并总结其优点,指出要改进之处。这一过程应用赞赏的眼光看待学生的作品。

完善感悟(2 分钟):学生通过吸取同伴作品的优点,不断完善提高。

以上所设计方案符合英语写作规律,符合英语学习循序渐进的学习规律,体现了任务型课堂教学模式,注重了英语学习的特点,培养了学生自主学习和合作学习的习惯,符合新课程标准的要求。

一、Teaching Plan for Continuation Writing(period Ⅰ)

Teaching Aims

After learning the lesson,the students are able to:

Sense and organize the different feelings during certain surroundings.

Teaching important points

Feeling changes and the expressions of excitement,inspiration and comfort

Teaching difficult points

How to continue writing according to the given text

Teaching strategies

Situation-based teaching

Task-based language teaching

Communicative approach

Teaching tools

Multiple media and Blackboard

Teaching procedures

Step one Lead-in

1. Show them a picture where an exciting event happens.

2. Have them discuss with partners their feelings in the exciting situation.

Step two

Learn the expressions about the feelings of excitement,inspiration and comfort:

1. Words and phrases

2. Sentences

3. A small discourse

(This is the most important step,where students can learn about the fine expressions of the feelings : excitement , inspiration and comfort . In the process , students can improve their writing abilities step by step.)

Step three

Read for structure

(Purpose:To develop students' abilities of organizing structures by going through the passage quickly to organize its structure and divide it into three parts in line with particular)

Step Four

Finish the continuation writing according to the given task.

Step Five

Present the students' assignments

Step Six

Evaluation(Ask the students to finish this evaluation.)

Step Seven Summary

二、读后续写教学设计(2 课时)——情景中表达同情、安慰、激励和激动的情感

个人情感的忧伤,情绪的低落,运气不佳,需要我们用恰当的方式对对方表达同情和怜悯,表示安慰和提供帮助。

安慰,宽慰指的是安顿抚慰,用欢娱、希望、保证以及同情心减轻、安抚或鼓励激励。可以侧重手的动作,也可以侧重眼神的信息传递;也可以在言语上进行安抚或者鼓励,等等。

激动、感动的心理特征是读后续写故事中常见的考点。这种心理活动常常和身体语言描写结合,如果再恰当地增加直接引语,就会生动形象地刻画出激动感动的画面。

(一)Build up linguistic Data

1. Words and Expressions

comfort	n. 慰藉;令人安慰的人或物 v. 安慰	relieve	v. 使减轻;使解除(痛苦、忧愁等)
considerate	adj. 体贴的;考虑周到的	relieved	adj. 感到宽慰的
excited	adj. 激动的	sensible	adj. 明智的;合理的;可觉察的
inspire	v. 激发,鼓舞	sensitive	adj. 善解人意的;(感情)敏感的

mercy	n. 仁慈;怜悯;恩惠;宽恕	sympathy	n. 同情(心)
moved	adj. 感动	thoughtfully	adv. 沉思地;体贴地
pity	n. & v. 同情;怜悯	thrill	v. 使激动 n. 激动;引起激动的事物
relief	n. (痛苦等的)减轻;宽慰	touched	adj. 感动

accept sb's sympathy	接受某人的慰问
at the mercy of	任······摆布,在······前毫无办法
be considerate to/towards sb.	对某人很体贴
be excited with/over/about	为······而激动〔兴奋〕
be inspired by	受······的鼓舞
be moved to tears	感动流泪
be sensitive to sb.	体谅某人
be sensitive to sth.	对某事敏感
bend down	弯下腰来
beyond one's expectations	出乎某人意料地
breathe/let out a deep sigh	发出深深的叹息
cast comforting glance at sb.	投去安慰的目光
express sympathy	表示慰问
feel sympathy for	同情······
hold back one's tears	控制住泪水
it was a pity (that)···	很遗憾
let sb. down	使失望;辜负
out of sympathy	出于同情
pat sb. on the shoulder	轻轻拍着肩膀
sigh with relief	如释重负地叹气
take pity on sb.	同情某人
without mercy	无情地

2. Situational Sentence Pattern

①Tears welled up in her eyes. 眼泪夺眶而出。

②A warm current rose in her heart. 一股暖流涌上心头。

③He was so thrilled that he could hardly speak. 他很激动,说不出话来。

④She could hardly contain her excitement. 她几乎掩饰不住自己的兴奋。

⑤I'm sorry to learn about the accident. 获悉此次事故,我深感悲伤。

⑥Let me convey my deepest sympathy to you.

允许我向您表示最深切的同情。

⑦Hearing the news, he jumped up and down with excitement.

听到消息,他高兴地跳了起来。

⑧The player jumped for joy when he scored the winning goal.

当他赢得获胜一球的时候,队员们兴奋地跳了起来。

⑨A slow smile worked its way across his face and into his eyes.

浅浅的微笑爬上他的脸,融进他的眼睛中。

⑩As Susan bent her head, she heard the remark and she wiped away tears.

当 Susan 低下头时,她听到了这句话,擦去了眼泪。

⑪She didn't say a word, but smiled a watery smile and held my hand tightly.

她一句话也没说,只是微微一笑,紧紧握住我的手。

⑫She stroked her fingers through my hair, and said, "Things are going to be fine."

她用手指抚摸着我的头发,说:"一切都会好的。"

3. Situational Text

Suffering from the failure of high jump at his second attempt, John collapsed to the ground, torn by sadness. A strong flood of sympathy welled up in my mind. Unable to bear his lack of hope, I paced towards him, patted him on the shoulder softly and conveyed my heartfelt comfort and encouragement.

(二)Finish the following with fine expressions according to the instructions

(1)他的眼泪落了下来,他奔向妈妈温暖的怀抱,对她说谢谢。(运用独立主格结构)

_____, he ran to mum's warm hug, and said gently, "Mum, thank you."

(2)我被他所做的事深深地感动了,泪水止不住地流下来。

①I was deeply moved by what he had done_____. (运用并列句句型)

②I was deeply moved by what he had done. _____. (运用独

立主格结构)

(3)妈妈建议我们在下一个路过的村庄搭帐篷,她的眼中闪着兴奋的光芒。

①Mom suggested that we go camping in the next village, _____ .(运用 with 复合结构)

②_____ , mom suggested that we go camping in the next village.(运用独立主格结构)

(4)难以抑制心中的兴奋,她高兴地跳了起来。

_____ , she jumped with joy.(运用形容词作状语)

(5)当她听到消息,她的心激动地怦怦跳。

①When she heard the news, _____ .(运用独立主格结构)

②When she heard the news, _____ .(运用 with 复合结构)

(6)妈妈朝湖边走去,然后传来一阵兴奋的尖叫声。(运用倒装结构)

Mom walked towards the lake, _____ .

(7)她哼着小曲,雀跃在林间。

She sang happily and _____ .(运用比喻)

(8)当看到圣诞老人走进来时,我女儿拍手鼓掌,高兴地上蹦下跳。(运用 and 并列结构)

When Santa walked into the room, _____ , my daughter

(9)接着从遥远的地方传来一个声音,这使我们沉浸在极度的喜悦当中。

①Then came a voice far from where we were, _____ .(运用非谓语动词结构)

②Then came a voice far from where we were, _____ .(运用定语从句)

Check up answers

1. Tears dropping from his eyes

2. and tears rolled down without control/tears rolling down without control

3. with her eyes glittering with excitement /Her eyes glittering with excitement

4. Unable to contain her excitement

5. her heart beating with excitement /with her heart beating with excitement

6. and then came an exciting scream/and then came a scream of excitement

7. skipped in the forest like a bird

8. clapped and jumped up and down

9. bathing us in extreme joy/which bathed us in extreme joy

（三）Finish the task according to the instructions

2022 全国新课标高考卷

阅读下面短文,根据内容和所给段落开头语续写两段,使之构成一个完整的短文。

It was the day of the big cross-country run. Students from seven different primary schools in and around the small town were warming up and walking the route(路线)through thick evergreen forest.

I looked around and finally spotted David,who was standing by himself off to the side by a fence. He was small for ten years old. His usual big toothy smile was absent today. I walked over and asked him why he wasn't with the other children. He hesitated and then said he had decided not to run.

What was wrong? He had worked so hard for this event!

I quickly searched the crowd for the school's coach and asked him what had happened. "I was afraid that kids from other schools would laugh at him," he explained uncomfortably. "I gave him the choice to run or not,and let him decide."

I bit back my frustration(懊恼). I knew the coach meant well—he thought he was doing the right thing. After making sure that David could run if he wanted,I turned to find him coming towards me,his small body rocking from side to side as he swung his feet forward.

David had a brain disease which prevented him from walking or running like other children,but at school his classmates thought of him as a regular kid. He always participated to the best of his ability in whatever they were doing. That was why none of the children thought it unusual that David had decided to join the cross-country team. It just took him longer—that's all. David had not missed a single practice,and although he always finished his run long after the other children,he did always finish. As a special education teacher at the school, I was familiar with the challenges David faced and was proud of his strong determination.

注意:

1. 续写词数应为 150 左右

2. 请按如下格式在答题卡的相应位置作答

> We sat down next to each other, but David wouldn't look at me.
> I watched as David moved up to the starting line with the other runners.

Discourse Analysis

本语篇属于"人与自我"—"生活与学习,做人与做事"主题语境下的"健康的生活方式,积极的生活态度",鼓励残疾学生参加越野赛跑的话题。

Time and Space Line

比赛日的当天,来自不同学校的孩子们要参加穿越茂密的常绿森林的越野赛。

Plot Line

文本以校际越野赛跑为线索展开。"我"是一名特殊教育教师,在越野赛跑当天,发现患有大脑疾病的 David 独自站在一旁,闷闷不乐。问其原因,他说准备放弃比赛。从教练口中得知,因为担心不同学校的同学们会嘲笑 David,教练想让 David 自己去决定是否参加赛跑。"我"让 David 追寻自己的内心,不理会别人的看法,David 最终参赛,尽管遇到困难,David 战胜了自己,这已经无关名次,而是他的勇敢和坚定让这一切成为可能。故事以第一人称进行叙述,全文结构清晰,情节环环相扣,衔接流畅。

Emotional line

文本故事是围绕着 David 参加越野跑展开。越野比赛日的当天我寻找David(期待)→看到 David 在篱笆边(疑惑为什么不进行准备活动?)→寻找教练,询问原因(理解)→再次找到 David(回忆 David 经历)→我了解 David(鼓励)→David 参加比赛(鼓起勇气)→比赛遇到挑战,没有放弃(意志坚强)→完成比赛,得到称赞(坚持不懈)。David 的残疾使得他对即将参加的校际越野跑产生畏惧,生怕学生们取笑他跑步的动作,对自己产生了怀疑。在老师的帮助下。他又重新找到自信,最后胜利完成比赛。这是突破自我,树立自信,坚持不懈,不断提升自己的过程。

Key Information

人物:文本中的人物有 David,"我"和 coach,但关键是 David 和"我"。

文本中的关键词有 :cross-country run, David, big toothy smile, afraid, laugh at, rocking, swung, a brain disease, run regular, participated, practice, finish, challenges, determination, proud 等。这些词汇在续写故事情节的形成和发展过程中,起着非常重要的作用,抓住了这些关键词就抓住了续写的思路。

Hint Sentences Analysis

由第一段提示句"We sat down next to each other, but David wouldn't look at me"可知,第一段可描写作者鼓励大卫继续完成比赛,大卫经过强烈的心理斗争,最终决定参加比赛。

由第二段提示句"I watched as David moved up to the starting line with the other runners"可知,第二段可描写大卫开始参赛,虽然中途遇到困难,仍然坚持到最后,完成了比赛。

Writing Ideas Building

续写的第一段,在我的鼓励下,David 走出了低谷,振作精神,决定参加比赛,我是如何鼓励他的? 我说了什么? 我做了什么? David 一开始不看我。听到我的鼓励之后,David 有什么反应? 他会说什么? 做什么? 这些都是学生思考的角度。通过语言描写和动作描写来呈现我如何鼓励他,以及他听到了鼓励内心斗争之后做出的决定。

第二段讲述 David 参加越野赛跑的经过和结果,而根据前文的铺垫,David 在跑步过程中遇到怎样的困难? 观看比赛的家长、老师和其他同学有什么反应? 是鼓励、呐喊,还是嘲笑? David 面对观众又会如何做出反应? 虽然落后别人很多,但是最终在众人的欢呼中完成了比赛。学生围绕文章的主人公展开适当的想象,最后他完成比赛,结尾可以升华主题。

Assignment Presentation

We sat down next to each other, but David wouldn't look at me. I looked at him softly, encouraging, "If it is because of others' attitude towards you that discourage you from running, I don't think it's a wise choice." He bit his lip, tears welling up in his eyes. It was when I was about to say something again that David raised his head, stared at me with determination and said firmly, "I'm going to run. !" He stood up and swung his feet forward to join the young athletes warming up there.

I watched as David moved up to the starting line with the other runners. With the sound of the starting gun, the kids rushed out, but David was immediately left behind. Even worse, he tripped and fell over. Seeing that, my heart missed a beat. I shouted encouragements, and out of expectation, cheers from the teachers, kids and parents erupted as well. David picked himself up and started again. The kids crossed the finish line one by one. After what seemed like a century, a tiny figure eventually appeared in the distance, with his body rocking from side to side. David made it —It was his run.

Evaluation

本文使用了行动类和情绪类的词汇: softly, encouraging, with

determination，firmly，expectation 等，动词的使用也很生动。高级句式有："It was when I was about to say something again that David raised his head，stared at me with determination and said firmly"（含有 It was…that 结构的强调句型），以及独立主格结构 with his body rocking from side to side 等。在叙述故事过程中，本文也很好地把握住了文中人物的性格特点。